# *You&Your*
# PARENTS

# *You & Your* PARENTS

## STRATEGIES FOR BUILDING AN ADULT RELATIONSHIP

## HAROLD IVAN SMITH

**AUGSBURG** Publishing House • Minneapolis

**YOU AND YOUR PARENTS**
**Strategies for Building an Adult Relationship**

Scripture quotations unless otherwise noted are from the Holy Bible: New International Version. Copyright 1978 by the New York International Bible Society. Used by permission of Zondervan Bible Publishers.

First names only are used with most of the stories told in this book. Unless otherwise noted, these names are fictitious and the specific details of the stories have been altered so as to make the characters unrecognizable.

**Library of Congress Cataloging-in-Publication Data**

Smith, Harold Ivan, 1947-
    YOU AND YOUR PARENTS.

    Bibliography: p.
    1. Adult children—Family relationships.  2. Parents
—Family relationships.  3. Parents, Aged—Family
relationships.  I. Title.
HQ755.85.S56    1987      646.7'8      87-17555
ISBN 0-8066-2267-9

Manufactured in the U.S.A.                      APH 10-7407

1   2   3   4   5   6   7   8   9   0   1   2   3   4   5   6   7   8   9

*This book is dedicated to all those of us
who occasionally lace up the gloves
and have a go at it!*

# Contents

# *Preface*

Recently, I had to go to the dentist. I decided that, as an adult, I didn't need a shot of Novocain. Afterward, the dentist and I both agreed that I should have had the shot.

For half an hour, I twisted and moaned and groaned, as the dentist tried to reassure me: "Just a bit more . . .," "I'm trying not to hurt you. . . ." The job had to be finished. That meant drilling until there was no more cavity. The healing could not begin until the hurting had ended.

The same is true of relationships between parents and their grown sons or daughters. Healing takes time. There are no psychological microwave ovens to speed up the process.

You may pick up this book and then conclude, "Oh, isn't this good for those who have this problem." But you may have this problem *yourself* and not realize it. Or you could *become* the problem for your children—in just a few years. The choices that you are making now could return to haunt you.

On the other hand, you might be someone who likes quick solutions, who puts a book back on the shelf if the answers don't appear by page 6. Some of the problems this book deals with have existed between parents and children for decades. How can you hope for instant solutions?

This book is for those who are willing to hang in there until the cavity is gone, for those who will not accept half-baked solutions to complex problems.

Believe me, after listening to so many people talk about their struggles with their parents, I wish I could offer answers that are "guaranteed to work or your money back." But that's just not the way relationships are.

If you give me a chance, though, I think I can offer some help. Perhaps things can never again be exactly the way they once were, but things can at least get better! To use Don Williamson's phrase, my desire for you is that you might find "closeness with distinct boundaries" with your parents.

# How Do We "Honor Father and Mother" Today?

Mother's Day. Father's Day. Two great opportunities to say "thank you" through brunches, flowers, cards, gifts, candy, and visits. These combine to make Mother's Day the second biggest commercial day of the year (Christmas is number one). If you have any doubts about that, try placing a long distance call on Mother's Day.

But for many people, these occasions and the family gatherings that go with them are bittersweet. Some spend hours looking for the right card—one that doesn't say *more* than the sender wishes. In desperation, some send a "white lie" and say to themselves, "I couldn't send a card that says what I'm *really* thinking." They offer kisses, hugs, and pleasant clichés while trying to ward off menacing thoughts.

When I was growing up we learned a game called, "Mother, May I?" The basic idea was that you couldn't advance without asking permission first. If you forgot and took a step or two, a playmate would scowl, "You didn't say, 'Mother (or Father) May I'!" Back to square one.

Many parents are repeating those words to their grown children: "You didn't say, 'Mother May I'!" The age of the son or daughter doesn't matter. Nor do the parents still need to be living in order for the accusing question to be heard. Some children hear their parents scolding them from the grave, like a "ghost of Christmas past" in Dickens.

Perhaps you don't have such a problem with your parents—at least not yet. But if you are married, it may be your in-laws that you or your spouse (or both) are having trouble with. The varieties of parent/adult child conflict are endless:

● Mary and Jim know it will start after Labor Day: the annual battle over Christmas plans.

● Beth refuses to visit her parents. She sends cards and flowers, but her parents want to see her under terms she cannot agree to.

● John feels guilty because he moved his mother into a nursing home. Over and over he mentally replays her angry statement, "Someday, you'll be old!"

● Don tries to be a peacemaker between his divorced parents, who are competing over their grandchildren. Grandmother never remarried and has adopted the role of martyr, while grandfather's second wife is only two years older than his son. Each grandparent tries to outdo the other on the grandchildren's birthdays and on Christmas.

● Kent feels the roles have gotten reversed. As his parents have aged they have become unstable, both emotionally and financially. He found his mother carrying $3000 in her purse.

● Joan and Herb fume every time his parents buy another outlandish gift for their children—without consulting them. The latest installment was a pony. The gifts also hurt *her* parents, who are retired and couldn't afford such items.

● Martha's parents have never forgiven her for her divorce—let alone her remarriage. In their view she is living in adultery with her new husband.

• Betty is annoyed every time her in-laws come to dinner. Her father-in-law and husband are in business together, and they never talk about anything that isn't work-related.

## *Understanding the Scripture*

Situations like the ones listed above are made even more complicated when we are satisfied with a simplistic understanding of Scripture. All our lives we have heard the commandment, "Honor your father and your mother, so that you may live long in the land the Lord your God is giving you" (Exod. 20:12).

Some of us learned the King James Version's rendering of that commandment, which is more severe: " . . . that thy days may be long upon the land. . . . " Either way, the impact of the commandment was increased when a parent put the emphasis on particular words.

Coming to terms with one's parents is not a new problem. Jonathan struggled with his father, Saul; Jesus had conflict with his mother, Mary; Esau struggled with his mother, Rebecca. While Saul's motives were sinister (to kill David), Mary's were not. Yet both parents complicated their sons' lives.

I can't prove it, but I suspect that if we could have interviewed the lost son (Luke 15) as he worked in the pigpen, some of his complaints would have sounded familiar, if not reasonable. When you read that story you may say, "If only *my* parents could be as open, as compassionate as *his* father was." But verse 15 says, ". . . while he was still a long way off, his father saw him. . . ." That's a good clue that *that* papa, too, had been wounded by alienation. He had probably contributed more to the alienation between him and his son than we might think.

What is remarkable about the father, though, is that when he saw his son, he ran to him. He didn't sit, with his arms folded, waiting for his son to grovel. He didn't have his "I told you so!" all prepared.

How many grown children are afraid to test the waters, to get beyond polite Sunday dinners and try for a real reconciliation?

Perhaps you *have* tried, but the stitches won't hold; the burden is too great for a Band-Aid. Or you may be bruised, and you'd rather leave things as they are.

Some parents do not know (or suspect) the real attitudes their children have toward them. Confrontations can be shocking: "I didn't know you felt that way!" When the truth starts to come out, so do some unhealthy types of reactions. Many parents fall into one of these categories:

● *Avoiders*. At the first hint of conflict, they flee—sometimes physically (to the bathroom or kitchen), sometimes verbally: "You know, I found the best recipe for blueberry cobbler in yesterday's paper. . . . " If they listen, they avoid comment.

● *Exploders*. Any hint of confrontation sets a match to their dry gunpowder. "I don't have to sit here and listen to this!" or "After all I've done for you, this is the thanks I get?"

● *Abusers*. These are exploders who break things or hit people.

● *Victors*. They are determined to win any conflict with their children. Some will rely on hierarchical models of the family. Some use sheer force of will to ensure victory; others use affection or trinkets.

● *Extinguishers*. These parents put out the conflict with as much water as possible. They don't want to leave any ashes smoldering for future flare-ups.[1]

"You haven't met my parents," one woman from Tacoma muttered as she read this list. Admittedly, the descriptions are very general and the list is not complete. But many people have recognized their parents' behavior pattern as fitting into one of these categories.

The commandment to honor your father and your mother has been a tough one for children in Christian families to deal with. After all, it's one of the Ten Commandments, so it can't simply be ignored.

But some parents have used Exod. 20:12 as a weapon. They have bruised their children with it just as surely as if they had been beating them with a baseball bat. Unfortunately, this misuse of the commandment has sometimes given angry children cause to walk away from both their parents and their faith.

Many adult children spend a great deal of emotional energy trying to sort out the messages they received from their parents while growing up. Child psychologist Jerome Kagan explained,

> . . . my own image of a life is that of a traveler whose knapsack is slowly filled with doubts, dogma, and desires during the first dozen years. Each traveler spends the adult years trying to empty the heavy load in the knapsack until he or she can confront the opportunities that are present in each fresh day.

What is the effect of the knapsack?

> Some adults approach this state, most carry their collection of uncertainties, prejudices and frustrated wishes into middle and old age trying to prove what must remain uncertain while raging wildly at ghosts.[2]

Parents have often had the privilege, through their wills, of saying to those who dishonored them, "You won't prosper long on the land. . . ." Altered wills and disinheritances have been a big part of our literature, movies, and family traditions.

## Real-life struggles

Ben Cartwright was the wise, old sage. Bonanza's father had Little Joe, Hoss, and Adam. These grown men were sons any father could be proud of. Oh, but look at the problems Miss Ellie has had with J.R. and Bobby. Or consider Blake Carrington's difficulties with Fallon and Steven.

Maybe we should bring back "Father Knows Best"—get Robert Young and Jane Wyatt back together again. They had the answers we need.

Why are television shows like "Dallas" and "Dynasty" so popular? Certainly it's not the depth of the dialog. I think it's because of the nerves that they touch and tease in us. We recognize ourselves in their struggles. The fact that they have a lot more money and power than we do just makes it more entertaining.

In recent years, television has given more attention to the problem of grown children coming home to live (with or without children of their own). "Maude" and "All in the Family" regularly touched the emotions of these situations. Millions of people have fathers-in-law like Archie Bunker. Some laughed on the outside, but winced on the inside. Some suspected that the scriptwriters had eavesdropped on their conversations.

Some of us have sat in living rooms or dens and watched episodes of such programs with our parents. Both the parent and the adult son or daughter probably hoped the other was listening. We have stolen glances, cleared our throats, wiped away tears, laughed—and then squelched it out of embarrassment. Why? Because the "situation comedy" was all too real.

## Unraveling the mysteries

The battles we wage in our families are long and complicated. Often it takes the help of a skilled counselor or psychologist to unravel the mysteries of parent/child relationships, to uncover what Eugene Kennedy calls the "clouded tales of life" from "the black and blue trauma of ordinary living."[3]

Tragically, some adult children do not get the counseling they need because they fear that any disclosure would dishonor their parents. The smaller the community and the more conservative the church, the less likely a person usually is to seek help from a counselor.

There are many factors that give each situation its own unique challenges:

• When all are Christians;

• When the adult children are Christians and the parents are not (or vice versa);

• When parents are more rigid in their interpretation of scriptural passages about relationships;

• When illness strikes the parents;

• When parents disapprove of their children's child-rearing practices.

John was thrilled when his alcoholic father quit drinking and made a commitment to Christ. But the "new" father wanted to make up for lost time, for the parenting he had never done. He didn't wait to develop spiritual maturity; he simply tried to seize power in a coup! There was no discussion, only: "My Bible tells me. . . ."

John's pleas of "But dad . . . " were fruitless. And the situation grew worse when John found out his father was making up for years of not giving to the church by sending money to TV evangelists whom John disliked.

Susan, John's sister, declared, "I'd rather have him this way than drunk." John argued with her, and so his relationship with his sister was affected as well. Now it was no longer alcohol that interfered with or threatened family gatherings, but religion. The family dynamics remained tense. Matt, the third sibling, became more estranged. Dad fought tooth and nail to bring him into line.

Dependency on our parents is a big factor for us. During our childhood years, it was our *physical* survival that was so closely linked to them. We quickly concluded, "Well, if these are the ground rules, so be it." As adults we are less physically dependent, but often still emotionally dependent on them. We cannot handle their faint praise or open criticism.

## *Spiritual talk*

Parent/child relationships are further complicated by parental clichés. Michele Slung calls them "momilies," or, "As my mother used to say. . . ." She notes, "Nothing seems to lodge in the mind so securely" as the well-turned parental phrase. Listen to yourself for awhile. How many times do you say, "My dad (or mom) always said. . . ." Michele Slung says:

> Momilies get repeated from generation to generation, and sometimes the original meaning is lost, yet the sense remains. Many of them are all-purpose, a few are cruel, the majority loving; what's amazing is how, year in, year out, they guide our behavior, in ways both large and small. . . . All you need to do is think of one of your mother's favorite sayings and her voice is magically in your ear. Whether you like it or not.[4]

Here are a few common momilies:

- "I'm *only* doing this for your own good. . . ."
- "If somebody else's mother lets him jump off the Empire State Building, would you want me to let you do it, too?"
- "Be careful what you wish for; you might get it!"
- "As long as you live under my roof, you will do as I say. . . ."
- "I'm not asking you—I'm telling you."
- "If I had talked to your grandmother the way you talk to me. . . ."
- "This is not a hotel. . . ."

Sometimes it's not the words or phrases themselves, it's the emphasis, the intonation or the exclamation mark that you clearly detect. Parents can still dust off these old phrases and use them to gain the attention of a child who is a CPA, MBA, or Ph.D.

In his book *Cutting Loose,* Howard Halpern includes a glossary of "saintly" expressions used by parents. Do any of these sound familiar?

● *always* ("We always go to church. . . .")

● *ashamed* ("I'd be ashamed of myself . . ."; "Aren't you ashamed?"; "You should be ashamed!")

● *best* ("I'm only thinking of what is best for you. . . . ")

● *God* ("God told me. . . .")

● *grateful* ("You should be grateful. . . .")

● *must* ("You must. . . .")

● *never* ("We never . . ." or "I never heard of such a thing!")

● *people* ("What will people say?")

● *if I were you* ("If I were you I would certainly. . . .")

● *shouldn't* ("You shouldn't feel/act that way. . . .")

● *shame* ("It's a shame the way he treats me!")

● *they* ("They say. . . .")[5]

And here are a few more: "Oh, really?"; "After all I've done for you . . ."; "The least you could do is. . . ."

Halpern makes this comment: "Some of us have been blessed by parents who are saints and we still may be trying to recuperate from this blessing."[6] Sometimes they don't even have to say anything. "They need only tilt their head at the right angle for their flashing halo to blind you to perceptions of reality other than theirs." Many parents become skillful at shaping words, expressions—even silences—into barbs. Many are masters of silence.

So why do we let these bother us? Halpern notes: "For many people, this early value system remains stable and unquestioned throughout life, with the person accepting the inevitable happy or unhappy consequences of that system."[7] However, through marriage, divorce, or a mid-life crisis, that entire system can get called into question.

## *Obstacles for evangelicals*

It's very easy for evangelical parents to try to bring their children into line through appeals to Scripture or spiritual authorities. They may rely on their interpretation of a particular passage to reinforce their position, or call on the authority of a pastor or Sunday school teacher. "What would Mrs. Hawkins say if she heard you?"

It's no wonder that some Christians are tied up in knots over their relationship with their parents. Just hearing one of the old code words (a "saintly" term) may bring back painful memories.

The issue becomes clouded because of our religious language. Very early, children learn to think of God as "Father." Sunday school teachers often talk about the fatherhood of God: "God is like your father." For many children, that evokes a comfortable image. But for others, the analogy is deadly: "Oh, no!"

The result can be some very negative attitudes about God, based on attitudes toward our earthly parents. Some children come to believe (even as adults) that they must earn God's love, that God's acceptance of them is only conditional:

"I love you *if*. . . . "

"I love you *when*. . . . "

"I love you *because*. . . . "

No wonder many Christians worry about losing their salvation. Their unconscious line of reasoning may go like this: *If dad stopped loving mom, he can stop loving me. If dad is like God. . . .*

Steven worked as a custodian in a large church while going to college. One day, as the senior minister of the church was passing by the sanctuary, he heard someone inside yelling, "You're just like my father! I hate you!" Then he heard loud sobbing.

It was Steven. His father was a traveling salesman and gone 80% of the year. Often he disciplined by phone. His mother would threaten Steven by saying, "Just wait 'till your father gets home!"

Our parents provide us with more than just our biological and (to a degree) emotional makeup; they are also transmitters of the seeds of faith. Some adults must struggle for many years with the nature of those seeds that are sown during childhood.

## Your adult agenda

The first item on your adult agenda is this: "What shall my relationship be to my parents?" This involves more than saying, "How long will the leash be?" Should there even be a leash? And what about the gray areas, those transitional times between childhood and adulthood, like college or post-graduate education or working in the family business? It's one thing to say, "As long as you're under my roof . . . ," but that may sometimes mean, "As long as you're cashing my checks . . ." or "As long as you work for me. . . . "

Relationships with parents influence divorce rates. How many people marry to get away from negative home environments? How many are desperate for love? for affection? for nurture? I believe there are *emotional* shotguns present at some weddings.

People have asked me, "Why are there so many divorces among people who have been married 20 or more years?" Part of the answer is that some of those people didn't have time to find a person whom they truly loved. They were pushed into an early marriage by anxious parents.

And how many pregnant girls married to "protect the family name," hoping they could make the best of a bad situation? Often, the resentment inside them rapidly grows.

The result is that thousands of divorced people blame their bad marriages not on themselves or on their mates but rather on their parents. But even so, few of them will put such accusations into words.

With the rapid increase in the divorce rate, many parents have declared "marital law" and have attempted to assume personal control over their children's marriages. Some checks or cash gifts have invisible (but real) strings attached.

## *What about you?*

What about it? Are you a grown-up child, or are you an adult son or daughter? It's *your* choice, not your parents'! Remember, Jesus faced problems with his parents, too. Has your family ever said, "You're out of your mind"? That's what his said about him (Mark 3:21). And they acted on their opinion. They "went to take charge of him." When they arrived, they waited. Then they sent someone in with a message: "Your mother and brothers are outside looking for you."

I find myself wishing that Mark had given more details. Did Jesus roll his eyes or groan? Did he grimace or rub his forehead? All we have is what he said. But it was an assertive response: ". . . he looked at those seated in a circle around him and said, 'Here are my mother and my brothers! Whoever does God's will is my brother and sister and mother' " (Mark 3:31-35).

Jesus' words about his family can still sound shocking to Christians today. But they must have started the whole town talking at the time. Jews took the commandment to honor father and mother much more seriously than we do, and the rabbis wrote long books of commentary to spell out just exactly how you were supposed to keep that commandment.

We have to assume that Jesus was making a point for his listeners (and for us) in Mark 3. He wasn't deliberately being rude. His words should be a caution to every Christian parent and child that what comes first in the family is not the question of power, but God's will in Christ.

## Growing old together

One reason why relationships with parents are more complicated today is that we are living longer. In Jesus' day, the life-expectancy was about age 35. In Colonial America, it was closer to 45. Today it is in the 60s and 70s, with women typically outliving men by a few years. Five generations within one family and golden anniversary pictures are no longer rare.

What's more, many older people are affected by medications. Some doctors prefer to give them prescriptions rather than listen to their complaints. We've got pills for everything. And if a senior has more than one medical problem, the interaction of these drugs can create even more problems.

The mother of a friend of mine has Alzheimer's disease. The daughter had to put her mother into a nursing home. The cost is enormous, involving financial sacrifices by the daughter. Often her mother calls and says, "You never come to see me!" These words have the effect of torpedoes on my friend's gentle spirit. Because of pseudoguilt, she hopped a plane and flew to see her mother, who didn't recognize her. Three days later her mother called again: "You never come to see me!" My friend was devastated.

Admittedly, many people "warehouse" their parents, saying, "They'll be happier with people their own age." But many also experience guilt for not personally caring for their parents.

Parent abuse has also increased. Grown children may take out their frustrations, resentments, and anger on their parents. Long-suppressed emotions incubate in their spirits. One "After all I gave up for you . . ." might be sufficient to push someone over the brink and strike back—physically.

Issues are emerging that weren't common 30 years ago: out-of-the-closet homosexuality, drug and substance abuse, abortion, live-in relationships, divorce and remarriage. Suppose a son comes home with his girlfriend and they want to sleep together in the guest bedroom? They may be 18, 28, 38, or 68. How does a parent respond?

And many adult children find themselves parenting their parents. One woman moaned, "My advice to my 70-year-old dad is the same as that to my 17-year-old son: 'Act your age!' "

Problems between parents and adult children are not new. Nor are they going to go away. But with some help, you can learn strategies that will help you to "honor father and mother" *and* build a responsible, adult relationship.

# *Overcoming the Five Fears*

Good farmers are experts in fertilizer. When I moved from San Diego to Kansas City, I was surprised by the number of fertilizer commercials on TV. I was used to seeing a barrage of ads for nacho chips, Sea World, cigarettes, and soft drinks. But I have learned that farmers don't just stick seeds in the soil and expect them to grow. First they *prepare* the soil.

That's the way it is with parent/child relationships, too. They don't grow in a vacuum. Some factors which influence the dynamics are visible, evident. Others lie planted in the fertile soil of the memory. Researchers estimate that by the age of 30, each of us has 3,000,000,000,000,000 pictures or memories. Many of those are positive. Many of them are neutral. Far too many are negative.

I have isolated five fears that influence our relationships with parents: fear of *change,* fear of *rejection,* fear of *success,* fear of *illness* or *dependency,* and fear of the *loss of dignity.* Our relationships can improve if we work to address and overcome these fears.

## *Fear of change*

Have you ever explored some of your family traditions? Someone may say, "That's just the way we've always done it." But suppose you do some detective work. How did that particular practice begin? Why did it become traditional? Was it originally a change from some other tradition?

John and Maria were immigrants to the United States. They came from Mexico, where John "ruled" the family. But here the power shifted, because Maria was the only one who knew English. She was the one who was in contact with the outside world. Two generations later, the family is a matriarchy. It became traditional for the women to lead.

Each generation should recognize that it has the right to re-examine family traditions. What has value in today's world? Fewer parents resist change when their children choose to adapt family tradition rather than reject it, thus preserving the best for the future.

You might come from a family where grown children are still expected to consult with mom and dad before making major decisions. But this tradition may be annoying to your mate. Perhaps you have had some verbal skirmishes over the issue. If the disagreement is not dealt with openly and constructively, it can emerge in the form of destructive confrontation: "Why didn't you stand up to them?" Many adults have felt trapped—torn between their loyalty to parents and to their mate. They see it as a no-win situation.

Carolyn Koons, director of the Center for Creative Change at Azusa Pacific University, has formulated five questions that are essential to consider:

1. Is there really a need for change?
2. Is the change better than what you now have?
3. Will it meet a certain need?
4. Does it come from within?

5. Have I anticipated the impact on me? on my parents?[1]

Look those questions over carefully. If you are facing a crisis or have an area of tension, relate the questions to it. Now relate them to the following situation:

Stuart talks fondly about his family's tradition of a "big Christmas, *together*." He has eight brothers and sisters; Stuart is the oldest. Only two siblings remain under mom and dad's roof. But now Stuart refers to the tradition his father holds dear as "Christmas chaos." "For two years we've tried to talk him into changing. There are seven in-laws and 13 grandchildren. We're talking about 34 people under one roof and with one bathroom. I don't know how he handled the 11 of us in one bathroom when we were growing up, but it won't work now. You practically have to make an appointment to use the john."

"What have you suggested as an alternative?" I asked.

"Oh, the church has a beautiful parlor and a big kitchen. It would be perfect for all of us but . . . ," he hesitated. "But I'm afraid of dad's reaction."

Now let's consider this situation in light of Carolyn Koons's questions:

Is there a need for change? Yes.

Is the change better than what they now have? There would definitely be more room and therefore more comfort and enjoyment.

Will it meet a certain need? Yes, the church has bathrooms, space for the smaller children to play, an automatic dishwasher, and would allow everyone to eat at one time instead of in shifts.

But question number four is the kicker: Does it come from within? In other words, has Stuart's dad thought up the idea? Stuart says, "Well, all of the kids agree it's the right idea. But we realize that dad will be dead set against it, possibly not even open to discussion or serious consideration. 'It wouldn't be the same.' "

Stuart developed a strategy for change. First, he praised the church facility. "Boy, I sure like that church parlor. Plenty of space."

Second, he gently planted the idea. "I was talking to Jim Cashman. You know, his family has gotten so big—they use their church parlor for their family Christmas get-togethers."

Third, he carefully analyzed his father's reaction. Although he rejected the idea, he was not as fierce as Stuart had expected.

Fourth, Stuart circled back and added data: "Cashman told me a funny story about the bathroom and how long he had to wait, and then the kids got into it. Really got on his nerves, all of them packed into the Cashman house. You know, it's not that big. Hey," he paused, "maybe we ought to think about something like that. . . ."

Then he waited for his dad to suggest the idea. Sure enough, next year, at Thanksgiving, his dad made the big announcement. "Now, I know some of you won't like this, but I think we'll learn to like it. . . . "

At Christmas, all during the big event in the church parlor, Stuart's dad chuckled about what a great idea he had had.

Why do we fear change? We fear it because:
● we have to give up the familiar.
● we have to replace it with the unknown.
● we open ourselves up to criticism.

If we recognize these fears and develop a strategy to overcome them, we may find that change isn't so difficult after all!

## *Fear of rejection*

Because of increased mobility today, children often no longer live within the "protective gaze" of parents. Others are still watched very closely. One of my neighbors is over 80 years old. Her daughter lives in the house on her right, her son in the house on her left.

- How far physically do you live from your parents?
- How far emotionally do you live from your parents?
- How far spiritually do you live from your parents?

Some parents make very little effort to change as they grow older. Their children come home and almost everything is still in exactly the same place. You look at the wall, and pictures are still there that were there 10, 20, 30 or more years ago.

John and Susan faced a dilemma. When they married, his parents gave them a painting that Susan hated. They dutifully hung it in their first apartment. When they bought their home in an affluent neighborhood, she drew the line. Naturally, when John's parents came for their first visit, they looked for the painting. Susan was hardly diplomatic. She simply said, "It doesn't fit the decor."

Sometimes no one wants to talk about why a gift or suggestion was rejected. We hope the givers will "take the hint," but some parents miss the cues. Preventing rejection of a gift from being interpreted as rejection of the giver requires good communication.

Allen is a minister who prefers Oxford cloth, button-down shirts. His mother shops at mill outlets and bargain stores. She buys him inexpensive, polyester shirts by the dozen. "You can't have too many good shirts," she reminds him. John never wears them but has never told her that he doesn't want them. Goodwill gets them.

Do some gifts that you have received end up never-worn, mildly appreciated, or given away?

Mary Thompson fumes at her grandchildren. "It has to be designer label or they won't wear it! We can't afford that stuff." Mary senses that her gifts to her grandchildren are not overly appreciated. She blames her daughter-in-law. "Howard certainly wasn't raised with a silver spoon in his mouth. It's all her doing. She's so uppity!" So every birthday, anniversary, and Christmas becomes a new occasion for insult.

With Elaine it was the doilies she made for her children. One day she happened to drop by unexpectedly, and her daughter had a garage sale going. She found the doilies. "Cheap, too," she added. An added insult was that her daughter lied about them later when she asked her what had happened to them. She didn't know that her mother had seen them at the sale.

But as painful as the rejection of goods or trinkets may be, the rejection of ideals is even tougher. Our values have deep meaning for us. My mom cried for three days when my brother registered to vote as a Democrat. I came home one day and said, "Mom, what's wrong?"

"It's your *brother*," she sobbed. *Oh, no,* I thought, *he's gotten some girl in trouble or been expelled from school or something.*

"What did he do?" I finally asked.

"He . . . he . . . registered *Democratic*." Later she blamed the high school teachers for it. "They brainwashed him. I know they did."

That was only the beginning. My brother and brother-in-law work for the same company my dad worked for. My dad was staunchly antiunion. Guess what my brother joined. Then came a strike, and my dad watched his son walk the picket line. That was hard for him to handle.

Some children reject their parents' work ethic. People of my dad's generation were fiercely loyal to a company. "LG & E, right or wrong." LG & E did not pay great wages, but in my dad's thinking it was "Steady work and no layoffs." But my brother's generation didn't think much of low wages. Similar conflicts have happened in families of American autoworkers whose children have bought imported cars.

Not wanting to be around one's parents is also a painful form of rejection. One son said: "It's not that we don't want to be around them, but . . . we're different. We go to symphony concerts; we pay $19.95 for a nice meal out. They don't understand."

Now listen to his father's viewpoint: "We're not good enough for them! Fancy-dancy places, spending money like it grows on trees. I've never paid that kind of money for a meal in my life."

The result was an impasse. Hurt feelings. I asked the son, "Have you ever invited them to go to the symphony?"

"They'd never go!" he snapped.

"But *have you asked?*" I insisted. He admitted that he had not. He was sure that they wouldn't spend that much money for good seats. "What about tickets to the symphony as a Christmas gift?" I suggested. "That would at least be a way to test the waters."

Another set of parents complained that their daughter seemed too busy to spend time with them. "She'll breeze in and say, 'Can't stay long, gotta go to. . . .' Imagine—she doesn't even have time for her own parents. That's *too* busy, if you ask me."

"They just don't realize how busy I am," the daughter explains. "My dad was a wage earner. He was home every day at 4:45, like clockwork. Sometimes I don't get out of my office before 6:00 or 6:30. Then there are clients to entertain, memorandums to read, and I'm involved in the singles group at church. Besides, they want me to sit there the whole evening while they rehearse all of their aches and pains and gripe about the injustices of the world."

It's clear that better communication could help *that* family, too. Fear of rejection is reasonable, yet also tragic. Many things are misunderstood because people are afraid to talk about them.

## *Fear of success*

Steve's dad is a funeral director—very straight-laced, and a little like some of the old stereotypes. Steve is just the opposite.

They are partners in a mortuary. When Steve was elected to the state board of funeral directors, you'd think his father would have been pleased. Hardly. It was competition that he couldn't handle.

"Social drinking," his father said to me. "He goes to those cocktail parties at the conventions."

"Sure I do," Steve admitted. "But I don't drink. You don't have to."

"But it hurts your influence," his father protested.

"Dad, I got elected to the state board. I have influence over our profession for the entire state."

Every meeting of the state board produced snide, cutting remarks. Steve didn't seek a second term. To keep peace in the family, he passed up a chance to be president of the state funeral directors association.

Some parents fear success that leads to material gain, and the comparisons that result. I have often wondered about Miss Lillian, President Carter's mother. She had two sons: one who lived in the White House, and one who ran a gas station and had his own brand of beer. How did she feel when she compared the two?

## *Fear of illness and dependency*

Most parents fear "being a burden" to their children. But when a divorce, a death, or an illness comes, they must often turn to a grown son or daughter.

"I hate to call Howard to come over and put up the storm windows," one mother says. "He's so busy. Sometimes he forgets, and I have to call and remind him."

"Nag, nag, nag!" Howard complains. "She must have called me every day. Finally I just dropped what I was doing and went over there."

Then Howard's wife spoke up. "I can say to him, 'This needs fixing.' Nothing happens. But when *she* calls, he drops everything to race over there."

It can be more complicated when an in-law thinks the parent has money and could pay to have the work done. I have a handyman friend who makes good money just settling family disputes by doing minor repairs, lifting, etc.

But serious, prolonged illness changes everything. Harry Petrakis wrote powerfully about this in his book *Reflections:*

> There were many times, especially as the weeks went on, when drugs and pain rendered him inert and silent, I'd sit beside his bed, trying to find something to say to reassure him and myself, yearning to leave so I would not have to see his veins, swollen and purple along his wrists, the pulse that wriggled like a small dark worm in his forehead. Worst of all was the smell of decay like a rank mist from his body. I couldn't understand how my mother endured the endless hours she spent with him. After sitting with him a while, I'd lie to him about an appointment or an errand that prevented my staying longer. He never complained about my departures, never tried to detain me, but urged me to go and meet my obligations. . . .
>
> On such a day, alone with him in the room, as I carried him the few feet from his bed to the armchair, he rested his cheek against my cheek. 'As I once carried you in my arms,' he said softly, 'now you carry me.'
>
> He died a few days later, quietly in his sleep, a short while after my mother had left the hospital to come home.[2]

Taking care of a parent can also be a financial burden. Or it may force decisions about where the parent will now live. If there has been repressed anger up to this point, living under the same roof may cause an emotional explosion. "Whose house is it, anyway?"

## *Fear of the loss of dignity*

What does it mean to be a parent who is now on Social Security and possibly a limited pension, and be unable to pick up the tab in a restaurant? unable to express affection by giving gifts?

How many senior adults have been taken into a son or daughter's home, only to be verbally or emotionally abused? The bruises are not on the outside, but on the inside. It doesn't always happen through statements like, "You're an inconvenience to us." There are other ways.

One parent raised the setting of the thermostat every time she passed it. Her son lowered it. The situation seemed less humorous when the next heating bill arrived.

Other children have said:

● "We can't go places. One of us has to be here all the time."

● "It's 'Bring me this, bring me that. I'm cold. I'm hot.' I have about had it up to here."

● "She doesn't like anything I fix. And if she gets in the kitchen, what a mess."

The sudden, unexpected illness of a parent can ignite fear in a son or daughter about their own future. It is a reminder that one day they may be in the same position of weakness. With the skyrocketing costs of medical care, can anyone feel comfortable about the prognosis of a slow, lingering illness?

## *Choosing to overcome*

The fears, failed attempts at communication, and conflicts so common between adult children and their parents are not inevitable. Reexamine your attitudes. What is reasonable change? What strategies can you develop to overcome the fears that prevent change?

The choice is yours. You can be satisfied with unresolved tensions or even open conflict, or you can make a decision to work toward positive, realistic change. The strategies outlined in this book can help you transform your desire for change into a reality.

# One

# Choose to Be
# a Son or a Daughter

In his book *The Sexual Dimension,* Herbert S. Stream says that many adults, particularly young adults, have formed a strong, "symbiotic bond" with one or both of their parents.[1] Often this has a negative effect on their ability to establish themselves as psychologically independent human beings.[2]

Teasingly, we talk about "mama's boys" and "daddy's girls," but when the child involved is age 23, 43, or 63, it's not that humorous. In some cases, sons or daughters have so identified with a parent that they are not able to marry successfully, or they may seek a mate who mirrors the earlier relationship—they look for a mama or papa number two.

## Emotional incest

Some adult children have been victims of "emotional incest"—when a parent deliberately creates an emotional (rather than physical), one-flesh relationship with a son or daughter. The emotional umbilical cord between parent and child is never severed.

Frequently this problem shows up between mothers and sons. It is natural for children to relate primarily to their mothers; a mother is the biological lifeline who nourishes a child during pregnancy, and after birth she is often also the primary caregiver. But this dependence has been complicated by the American tradition of fathers becoming immersed in their work, leaving little time for close interaction with their children. In many cases fathers fade into the background and their sons must try to identify with elusive, shadowy role models.

Herb Goldberg points out that when a father *does* make an impact on his son, it is often as "the heavy"—in the role of punisher: "Just wait until your father gets home and hears about this!"[3] Frequently fathers are so distant that their sons must rely on their mothers to teach them what it means to be a male.

This situation has become even more significant with the growing number of single-parent homes—90% of which are headed by women. Judges have traditionally granted custody to the mother unless it could be proven that she was unfit. (Interestingly, this has been customary in America only since 1815. Prior to that, it was assumed that a child's natural place was with the father.)

The problem of emotional incest has been increased by the greater numbers of adult singles living at home with their parents. We tend to assume that marriage is what defines adulthood. We ask singles, "When are you going to settle down and get married?" The tone of the question suggests that a single person is somehow not an adult. Some religious authorities teach that children should remain under the strict authority of their parents until they marry.

Many of the 34 million never-married single persons in this country reject this view, and choose either to live by themselves or with one or more roommates. This fosters a healthy transition from childhood into adulthood. But even then, it is surprising to discover how many parents have keys to their children's apartments, condos, or houses.

## *Tasks of early adulthood*

Robert J. Havinghurst has identified eight developmental tasks that society assumes should take place during early adulthood:[4]

1. Selecting a mate
2. Learning to live with a mate
3. Starting a family
4. Rearing children
5. Managing a home
6. Getting started in an occupation
7. Taking on civil responsibility
8. Finding a congenial social group

We have often thought that adults would start with the first task and work their way down the list until all had been achieved. Then they would be ready for the responsibilities of middle adulthood.

However, several factors have interfered with this ideal scheme. The first is the upward mobility of the American people. For example, most parents in the '60s and '70s wanted their children to get a "good education," which usually meant at least some college. Many wanted their children in professional fields: nursing, law, dentistry, medicine, accounting, religion—which required even more education and longer delays in some of the items on the agenda.

The sexual revolution also had an effect. Once it was generally assumed that a man would not marry until he could support a wife. But when "the pill" arrived on the scene and premarital sex became more widespread, many parents became frightened. Instead of asking their children, "How are you going to support a family?'' they started asking, ''When are you going to get married?'' Long engagements were discouraged.

But many couples could not afford to get married without some help from their parents, and so the umbilical cord was strengthened or, if it had been severed, reconnected. At Vanderbilt I wrote my graduate thesis on college student marriages. I was surprised by how many of these couples were still getting checks from home. Many of the checks had strings tied to them, however.

## Renegotiating the parental relationship

It seems to me that the priority item of adulthood is not marriage, but renegotiating the parental relationship. Jesus was quoting the book of Genesis when he said, '' 'For this reason a man will leave his father and his mother and be united to his wife, and the two will become one flesh' '' (Matt. 19:5). To ''leave'' one's father and mother also involves leaving behind the kind of emotional bonds that can interfere with the new bond between husband and wife.

The Genesis text outlines three tasks:
1. to leave;
2. to be united;
3. to become one flesh (Gen. 2:24).

Scripture does not call for an *amputation* of parental ties, but for gradual *emancipation* from them. However, even this has become a difficult task because of our modern patterns of family life.

The close relationship between mothers and their children has been reinforced by work shifts and travel schedules that have taken husbands and fathers away for long periods of time. A significant number of mothers have spent more time talking with their children than with their mates. It should be no wonder that we have empty nest syndrome in this country, especially where a marriage has been held together primarily "for the sake of the children." We have a nationwide pattern of *child-centric* marriages rather than *paircentric* marriages.

So if a wife has not developed a strong emotional or spiritual relationship with her husband, she may naturally turn to her children. Carole Klein suggests that when some women discover the inadequacies of their husbands, they turn their attention to their sons—to help their sons grow up to be the men their mothers wish their husbands had been. Many women have grafted their own ambitions—unattainable because of their sex—onto a son. "In fact, when there is a bitter marriage to contend with, the bleakness may serve to fuel a son's ambition, for he wants to make up to his mother for his father's failure. The son will, by his fame and success, put pride back into his mother's life."[5]

Abraham Lincoln once said, "All that I am, I owe to my darling mother." Many other men could have said the same thing. Klein's study noted that it was the rare man of accomplishment who did not give at least some degree of the credit to his mother's influence. At the same time, many of them have struggled with trying to live up to their mother's expectations. One successful salesman complained, "No matter what I did, what accomplishments I laid at her feet, I always felt it wasn't enough!"[6]

Here are just a few of the mothers whose close relationships to their sons had much to do with their success:

● Caroline Fleuriot Flaubert lived with her novelist son Gustave Flaubert throughout most of his life. He once wrote her, "I know very well that I shall never love another as I do you. You will never have a rival, never fear."

● Margaret Morrison Carnegie was so devoted to her son, industrialist Andrew Carnegie, that he promised her he would never marry while she lived. He kept his word. He finally married at age 51, six months after her death.

● Sara Delano Roosevelt never stopped trying to dominate the life of her son, Franklin D. Roosevelt. When he married and moved to Boston, she rented a house near the couple; then she gave them a house, attached to hers. When he was asked to run for governor of New York, he told political leaders he would have to consult with her first.

● Jessie Wilson's son, Woodrow Wilson, joked that he had been tied to his mother's apron strings "till I was a great big fellow." Wilson was the president who signed the resolution proclaiming Mother's Day.

● Mary Hardy MacArthur accompanied her son Douglas MacArthur to West Point. When he was assigned to guard duty, she often accompanied him. He once told a president that he could not accept a military command because of his mother's ill-health. As general of the Army, he would go home to eat lunch with her.

● Annie Hoover lived with her lawman son J. Edgar Hoover until her death at age 80. He remained a bachelor throughout his life.

● Rebekah Baines Johnson taught her son Lyndon B. Johnson to read at two, and had him reading Longfellow by age three. In order to have extra time with him, she often accompanied him as he walked to school.

The list could go on and on. Certainly each of these women made a profound impact on the world through her relationship with her son. But if such successful men had difficulty disengaging themselves from their mother's attentions, we shouldn't be surprised if we have problems with our own parents.

### *"I'll be here if you need me!"*

That heart-stopping feeling parents get when the nest is empty lies at the root of many problems between them and their adult children. Parents become used to being needed for money, advice, Band-Aids, ironing, or chasing away boogeymen. They develop reflexes that look a lot like the U.S. seventh fleet in action. Every time there is trouble in the Middle East, the seventh fleet ships out and cruises around the Mediterranean—"just in case."

A son or daughter's attempt to be more independent may wound parents. How many of them can accept the fact that their children can get along all right without their help? How many of them are willing to let their children have enough freedom to stub their toes?

Many children have kept their keys to their parents' houses. During the last recession, thousands of adult children went back home. Many of them are still there. One woman wrote:

> Caught in the economic crunch, three of our adult children are once again residing in the family homestead. None of them can afford the down payment on houses in our area or the high interest rates, and the local apartment rates are prohibitive. There is no way any one of the children can afford to set up housekeeping, and we are unable to subsidize them. We have a problem.[7]

In the book of 1 Samuel, David's problems with King Saul were complicated by the fact that he had become Saul's son-in-law. In fact, Saul had used his daughter, Merab, as bait to win David's loyalty and get him killed in battle. When that relationship fizzled, Saul was delighted to discover that another daughter, Michal, was in love with David. He was pleased. "I will give her to him . . . so that she may be a snare to him" (1 Sam. 18:20-21).

David resisted that, saying, "Do you think it is a small matter to become the king's son-in-law? I'm only a poor man and little known" (v. 23). So Saul arranged for the bridal price to be scaled down to what David was able to pay. He demanded the foreskins of 100 Philistines; David promptly brought back 200 of them. When Saul realized how much Michal loved David, he became even more afraid of him (vv. 23-29).

It's not that some parents deliberately seek to sabotage their children's relationships, but their loyalty is to their children. Just before one daughter began to walk down the aisle at her wedding, her mother told her, "I'll leave your room just the way it is—anytime you want to leave him."

Have *you* been a victim of emotional incest? Have you allowed a parent to come between you and the vows you made to a mate? Have you allowed hairline cracks to develop in your marriage by trying to please your parents on a particular issue?

Perhaps it's time you renegotiated your relationship with your parents. You can choose to be a son or daughter by redefining your relationship. It may be difficult, because entrenched habits are hard to break. But an adult relationship with your parents requires a willingness to cut the apron strings. Maybe it's time you looked for the scissors.

# Two

# Reject Your Parents' Fears and Irrationalities

My dad used to bring home big cardboard boxes in which sets of four electric housemeters had been shipped. With my boyish creativity I made all kinds of things out of those boxes—tunnels, firehouses, stages.

My mother had a big, wooden-handled butcher knife that was "perfect" for cutting doors or whatever else was needed in that thick cardboard. One day when I was four years old, my grandmother came to visit. I was playing out on our big back porch, and all of a sudden my grandmother started shrieking hysterically, "My God, Mary! The boy's got a butcher knife!" My mother casually nodded and went about her work. Then my grandmother went into an anguish-laden litany of all the dire consequences that *could* happen to me.

That day my mother taught me a valuable lesson: Sometimes you have to reject your parents' fears.

Recently I asked my mother about that incident. While she did not remember the specifics, she well knew her mother's history of anxiety. She said, "You know, when I was young, we lived so far out in the country, she was always afraid we could cut ourselves and bleed to death." But my mom and dad lived in the city, and my mother had supervised enough of my previous experiences with the knife so that she trusted me to be careful. She knew that those hours spent on the back porch nourished my creativity. We didn't have a lot of money to buy "store-bought toys," so we had to improvise.

I realize now how much courage it took for my mom to ignore grandmother's prediction, "You mark my words, he'll cut his throat!"

## Emotional heirlooms

It isn't easy to reject a parent's fears and irrationalities. Like prejudices, they are passed on from generation to generation. We need to take a critical look at some of the emotional heirlooms we have inherited.

● Some parents are *protective*. They don't want to see their children (or grandchildren) hurt. They know that it's a cold, cruel world out there.

● Some parents are *covetous*. They fear that if you fly too high—without a safety net—you might fly away. So they give vent to their fears in order to control you or to sabotage your ambitions.

● Some parents are *predictors*. They are right there when you fail, saying, "I told you so," or worse.

In his novel *Rivington Street,* Merideth Tax portrays the relationship between a banker father and his son, who lived in New York after the turn of the century:

> William Sloate . . . had plans for each of his children and had let them know what was expected of them. . . . Denzell's assignment was more vague; he was to be a credit to the family.

William was concerned with anything that might harm Denzell

or hurt the family's reputation, such as Denzell's love for the newly-invented airplane.

> Denzell tried to convince his father that this hobby was of potential use. Someday aeroplanes would be used for transportation, mail, hunting, racing; they might even be adapted by the military in the unlikely event of another war. But his father was adamant. . . .
>
> "It's too dangerous. As long as your money is in my control, you'll have to stay out of those things!"[1]

Sound familiar? I can remember a few conversations with my dad that went like that.

A friend of mine was offered an opportunity to go to Europe and the Holy Land. She called me.

"What am I gonna do?" she asked.

"About what? It's a great price. Go!"

"But my mother is threatening to die while I'm gone." (For years her mother had used this approach to manipulate her.)

I said, "Tell her that if she dies they'll be able to keep the body until you get back. And tell her that someone else will get the souvenirs you bring home for her."

My friend was torn, but eventually she left for Europe. Her mother survived by photocopying news articles about the hijacking of the TWA jet at Athens airport. "Don't say you weren't warned!" she wrote on them.

Then there is Sally, who wanted to sing opera. Eventually her ambition took her away from the small, Illinois farm town where she grew up, all the way to New York City. Her mother moaned, "You'll get mugged! Raped! Or worse!" And the tone of her voice communicated the message, "You won't sing gospel music anymore. You'll sell out."

Sally did get mugged—twice. But she also provided a Christian witness among musicians in New York. And as her career has advanced, she has become an unofficial "den mother" to many Christian musicians who have moved to the "Big Apple."

Sally's mother came to see her in New York once. After she heard her daughter sing, her only comment was about the "cut" of the gown. "Too much cleavage," she said. Sally was devastated. By New York standards, the dress was puritanical.

Michael taught school for four years, but daydreamed of writing. "Being a teacher is a good thing," his father said. "Three months vacation—that's when you can write."

"But it's unpaid vacation," he reminded his dad. "Besides, I want to write all the time—not just in the summers."

His father's response was, "You can't have your cake and eat it too."

When Michael made up his mind to quit teaching, his father denounced both him and his decision. "It's stupid! What kind of a son have I raised that would quit a good job. You've got paid Social Security, hospitalization, tenure, two weeks at Christmas. . . ."

Michael quit his job anyway. His father was right about it being a financial sacrifice, but it also brought Michael a deep sense of peace and satisfaction.

His dad, however, hasn't let him forget it. He says things like, "Your sister is skiing this week. . . . I took a ride in your brother's *new* car. Nice!"

Marge is a single parent who has struggled with her own parents. Her youngest son is small for his age but big in desire. Marge let him play football, and that angers her parents. "He's going to get hurt. He's too small!" the grandmother warns.

Barb, Marge's friend, has the opposite problem. Her son has no interest in athletics but a strong interest in science and reading. "You're making a sissy out of him," her mother thunders.

But Barb knows that her boss, a brilliant scientist, was like her own son at that age. And he was able to succeed because *his* mother persevered against strong pressure from grandparents, letting him be his own person.

## *Saul and Jonathan*

King Saul turned against David, "because the Lord was with David but had left Saul" (1 Sam. 18:12). Here the principle of transference was at work. Saul's real problem was with God. He couldn't fight God, but he could try to stop David.

All David had done was kill a giant that Saul had had ample opportunity to kill. But the last straw for Saul was when the women of Israel came out and sang, "Saul has slain his thousands, and David his tens of thousands" (v. 7). Saul was overcome with the irrational fear that David would take the kingship. He said, "What more can he get but the kingdom?" Saul hurled his spear at David, saying, "I'll pin him to the wall." But David ducked (vv. 9-11). Finally, Saul "told his son Jonathan and all the attendants to kill David" (19:1).

Now Jonathan was faced with a personal crisis. He had a commitment to Saul both as a king and as a father. And as a potential heir to the throne, Jonathan would have benefited by having David eliminated. Yet "Jonathan was very fond of David" (v. 1). So he warned him: "My father Saul is looking for a chance to kill you. Be on your guard tomorrow morning; go into hiding and stay there. I will go out and stand with my father in the field where you are. I'll speak to him about you and will tell you what I find out" (vv. 2-3).

Jonathan kept his word. Not only did he reject his father's irrationality, he openly challenged it:

Jonathan spoke well of David to Saul his father and said to him, "Let not the king do wrong to his servant David: he has not wronged you, and what he has done has benefited you great-ly. He took his life in his hands when he killed the Philistine. The Lord won a great victory for all Israel, and you saw it and were glad. Why then would you do wrong to an innocent man like David by killing him for no reason?'' (vv. 4-5).

It took great courage for Jonathan to make that statement. Kings don't like people telling them they made the wrong decision. But his father listened to him. And as a result, ''David was with Saul as before'' (v. 6). But the story did not end there. Jonathan had failed to realize how deeply rooted were his father's fears.

## Confronting your parents' fears

You will probably not diffuse your parents' irrationality about a particular issue in one discussion, even if you go into the conversation ''loaded for bear.'' It takes time and patience. Also, the higher the verbal volume level, the less effective such encounters are. In their book *The Joy of Working,* Denis Waitley and Reni L. Witt offer some helpful suggestions:

1. Stick to the subject.
2. Have the subject clearly delineated in your mind.
3. Never trample on the other person's ego. (Sarcasm, in-sults, and intimidation can boomerang.)
4. Sidestep any attempt by the parent to belittle you.
5. If the conversation heats up, stay calm. If necessary, call for a time-out.
6. Be prepared for concessions. Determine ahead of time what you can live with.
7. Under no circumstances give away something that is ab-solutely essential to you.[2]

You do not have to "win" just because your parents lose the argument. One of the reasons there was a World War II is that the peace agreement ending World War I treated the Germans so harshly. A positive, constructive outcome requires that you plan ahead, anticipating your parents' responses. And be sure that you ask God to help pave the way for you.

Before rushing into a confrontation, spend some time analyzing whatever it is that feeds the irrationality. *That's* the enemy—not your parents. Seeing your parents as the enemy is the way to win the battle and lose the war.

Changes require time. Some of your parents' fears are deeply entrenched, and your parents have become comfortable with them. They may have been valid at some time in the past or may have applied more to one of your siblings.

Finally, remember that some of our parents are products of the Great Depression of the '30s. They learned not to be risk-takers, and to opt for security when they had the choice. They believe it is better to be safe than sorry. For those of us who know the Depression only through oral and written history, it's hard to understand the pain it inflicted, the dreams it destroyed. But to a generation that remembers soup kitchens and cardboard stuffed in the bottoms of their shoes, being financially insecure is frightening. And those old fears parents have are mingled with the love and good intentions they have for their children.

So how do you tactfully reject those fears and irrationalities? Here are some suggestions:

● Point out that you are rejecting their fear—not them!

● Don't belittle the fear, saying, "That's silly!" It may be silly to you, but in their own experience or way of thinking it probably makes perfect sense.

● Recognize and understand the fueler of the fear.

● Listen and consider what they say before you respond or react.

● Be gentle in triumph. Don't rub it in.
● Remember that you are an adult son or daughter, not a child.

# Three

# Determine Your
# Territorial Waters

The United States takes the position that its boundaries extend 200 miles offshore. Beyond that point lie "international waters," where anyone can fish and where international law prevails. There have been many confrontations inside that 200-mile limit, when a fishing boat or other vessel has been seized by the Coast Guard.

A country's airspace, too, is carefully guarded. A Korean airliner was shot down near the border of the Soviet Union because it had crossed into that nation's airspace. Some governments are inclined to shoot first and ask questions later.

So it is with the "turf" between parents and their grown-up sons and daughters.

- Are there topics you prefer not to discuss?
- Are there subjects you definitely avoid?
- Do your parents respect those limits? Do they test your territorial waters?

Some parents cannot conceive of such a thing as an off-limits subject with their children. One parent may be more sensitive and warn the other, saying, "Now Charles, I don't think we need. . . ." In many families, she is interrupted by a verbal or visual put-down from Charles that says, "Mind your own business."

Where boundaries are not respected in families, battles break out. Sometimes family members beat a hasty retreat from dining room tables or living rooms or front porches. In other families things get broken—if there isn't a family diplomat to step in and quickly mediate a truce. Too often, wounds are opened up but there is no opportunity for closure.

The "hot" issue may be politics, religion, the role of women, money, or childrearing. Whatever it is, it sets off the emotional geiger counters.

In hierarchical families dad may come to a conclusion and expect everyone else to "toe the line." Often there is a family rebel to challenge the edict.

Other families operate with a strategy of compromise ("This time, please. . . ."), for the sake of family unity. But saying, "Just this one time" can become a habit. And if the fuse is finally lit (perhaps by an outsider, such as an in-law), watch out.

Many family gatherings require people to walk around for hours on tiptoes, with everyone trying to avoid a certain subject, and no one wanting to be the one who spoils the occasion.

## Long-term patterns

It is important to remember that these family patterns are long established and therefore not easily adjusted. If you are an outsider, you may not be able to recognize the subtle nuances. Why, for example, is rebellion permitted in just one child? "Oh, that's just Ben. . . ."

Often the temperature gets raised by family members engaging in name-calling, accusations, double-teaming, or dragging in old history. You may hear statements such as,

- "That's the dumbest thing I've ever heard of."
- "Oh yeah, how would you know?"
- "What makes you so smart, Mr. Know-it-all?"

When this happens, even insignificant discussions can become breeding grounds for resentment. The consequences of the discussion remain long after the issues are forgotten. An individual may have been proven right or wrong, but the put-downs are what make the lasting impression.

Some families feel it necessary to call a truce for Christmas or for a family reunion. One mother says that on Christmas Eve she finds herself anxiously wondering "whether this will be one of the good years."[1]

A family gathering can easily become a battlefield. Dr. Donald Bloch observed, "Unresolved family issues can be ignored or swept under the rug for most of the year, but people are forced to pretend (at holidays)—in a configuration of joy and happiness—that everything is all right and it isn't all right."[2] Suddenly someone with whom you have unfinished business is under the same roof with you. Some houses don't contain enough square feet to keep the confrontation from occurring.

Often the problem is that family members don't hear what one another are saying. Some families can use only high-pitched tones. Someone thinks they have heard what the other person said, and then jumps in. People talk *at* each other rather than *to* each other.

Perhaps you grew up in a family like Maria's. Everything merited a personal opinion. A color was not just white: it was either antique white or oyster white. Which was it? In such families you are not permitted the option of saying, "I don't know and I don't care." Opinions must be made specific, and that fuels the arguments.

## Managing to be diplomatic

My dad was a lifelong Republican and loved Herbert Hoover. In college history classes I had learned about Hoover's foot-dragging as the Depression began, and at my graduation I happened to offer my "humble" opinion on Hoover's effectiveness as a president.

"What would you know, sonny boy?" my father demanded. "You weren't even born then!" Ah, but I had a B.A. in American history. My mother quickly intervened by changing the subject. The point is this: some issues are not worth fighting over. They are energy-drainers. Moreover, it is possible that they will produce more heat than light. So how do we manage to be diplomatic?

*1. Sometimes we must filter.*   I have to remember that my dad spent 40 years working for the same company, and he had to deal with a flock of "college boys" who came in and took over management. Some of their "textbook" ideas and solutions were ridiculous. So a college degree was not proof to him of knowledge or intelligence.

*2. Sometimes one has to ignore minor irritants to focus on major ones.*   That's why fire departments have a fire-classification system: one, two, or three alarms. They know how to distribute resources. Part of being an adult is ignoring some issues even when another adult insists on using them to bait you.

*3. When we disagree, we still honor.*   Emotion-laden phrases like, "You're crazy!" are inappropriate on both sides. Just because your father calls you dumb doesn't mean you have to fight back. Part of what it means to respect each other is to be concerned about our tone of voice, our pitch, and our intensity.

*4. We warn people when they are on thin ice.*   In international waters, warning shots are expected—across the bow of the ship. That was the major reason for the outrage when the Soviets shot down the Korean airliner—they gave no warning. All we need to do is say, "I am getting uncomfortable with this topic." You could also be more direct: "Could we change the subject, please?" Or it could be a good time for a bathroom break, even if you don't need to go to the bathroom. Indoor plumbing has cooled down many hot tempers.

*5. Check the control motive.*    In some families, territorial boundaries have become fuzzy because of how much money adult children owe their parents. Parents feel forced to comment or editorialize, the same way a bank would express concern to a heavily-indebted business about some of its practices. In some families there is the prospect of money "down the road." Parents attach strings to their plans for benevolence.

*6. Check the power motive.*    Three generations of Joneses attend one Baptist church. They are a powerful family—as each new pastor has discovered. Jones *Sr.* has controlled the church for years. It is as if he holds "power of proxy" over his grown children. When he decides he doesn't like the pastor, soon he has Jones *Jr.'s* support, and so on until the entire family is behind him.

Only God knows how many churches have been split and torn by power-broker families, or how many offspring have been caught in the cross fire. In some churches, there may just be too many people with the same last name.

*7. Insist on freedom.*    Many parents have tried to legislate their ambitions onto their children and their children's children. For example, Rob gave in to his father and attended dental school. But two years after his father's death, he sold his practice to start a different career that he knew was what he really wanted to do.

What about you? Have you felt parental pressure or actual interference in your career plans? Or in those of a brother or sister? Have you abdicated your dreams in order to keep parental support?

*8. Be alert to sibling feuds.*    You may not have a problem with your parents until they try to draw you in on their side in a fight with one of your brothers or sisters. Ask yourself, "Is this *my* battle? What are the consequences if I jump in? If I don't get involved?"

*9. Remember, in-laws have territorial waters, too.* Sometimes sibling feuds influence in-law relationships. That's what happened with Jacob and Esau. Rebekah had shown favorites and helped Jacob steal his father's blessing. Esau held a grudge against him because of it. He didn't actively rebel against his parents, but he knew how to annoy them. When he was 40 years old, he married Judith and Basemath, who are described as "a source of grief to Isaac and Rebekah" (Gen. 27:41). Sensing how annoyed his mother was, he went on to marry Mahalath, the daughter of Ishmael (28:8-9). If anyone had problems at a family reunion, it would have been that family.

Many spouses are wounded by friction with their in-laws. If a wife has grown up in a family where women are encouraged to form and express opinions, what happens if she dares to disagree with an outspoken father-in-law, who believes that women should be seen and not heard? How will the husband react if his father verbally belts his wife? She has crossed over into that family's territorial waters.

At times like these, we can easily forget a marriage vow to "forsake all others."

Susan complains, "Jim never sticks up for me. Going home in the car, he will admit I was right, but he won't stand up for me. If I say something is blue, then just for meanness his father will say it's purple. And Jim will just sit there. Just once I wish he would stick up for me. He says, 'You gotta understand my dad.' Baloney!''

## Overlapping loyalties

In 1 Samuel 20, Jonathan did not want to accept the fact that his father, King Saul, was trying to kill David. His friendship with David overlapped with his loyalty to his father. David noted, ''Your father knows very well that I have found favor in your eyes, and he has said to himself, 'Jonathan must not know this or he will be grieved' '' (v. 3). David had already escaped two new attempts on his life (19:10-12).

I wonder if Jonathan thought that somehow this territorial fight would resolve itself. He himself had once been ordered to kill David, and yet he wanted to believe that his father had changed his attitude (20:2,9). As Chapter 20 proceeds, Jonathan's use of exclamation marks is very notable as he tries to convince David (and himself) that everything is OK. Obviously the tension was building up in him over where the boundaries were.

The territorial waters issue can be tough—especially if you are the oldest child, the first out of the nest. Your parents are dealing with these issues for the first time, so it's easy for them to make mistakes. But if you choose not to blaze a trail as you go, your younger brothers and siblings may have to struggle too. By working through these issues now, you will be doing them a favor.

Some parents will use inappropriate tactics to try and get their way. So you may have to settle for small victories. It may be that real change will come only after a long series of skirmishes. If you find yourself on the receiving end of abuse, you may have to say, ''I refuse to be hurt *today* by my father (or mother).''

In his fine book *Growing Together,* John Trent offers some insights into communication that are helpful with parents as well as in a marriage relationship:

● I am always communicating—even when I think I am hiding behind a wall of silence.

● Both my words and my nonverbal actions need to communicate the same message. Otherwise the other person may be more confused and more resistant.

● I must not allow other troublesome relationships to interfere with this communication.

● When we are having a serious talk, maintaining close physical contact is helpful. (Look your parents in the eyes.)

● The gift of not interrupting is part of the respect that I owe.

● Even when difficult, I will communicate in a clear and direct manner.

● Both my parents and I are responsible for initiating communication.[3]

To Trent's list I would add: Keep careful control of your vocal response.

You and your parents always have the option of developing a new way of communicating. Maybe there have been verbal melees in the past, but that doesn't mean today's conversation has to follow that script. *You* need to be responsible for working at communicating clearly with your parents.

You may have to remind your parents, "Would you please listen all the way to the end of a sentence?" But remember that such listening could be frustrating for them (if you are rambling) or even painful (if you are bringing back difficult memories).

There will be times when your parents will disagree with each other about what they think you said, and both of their opinions are different from what you thought you communicated. Ask questions to make sure they are hearing what you intend.

Commend your parents when they make some progress, no matter how small: "I really appreciate it when you listen to me. When you give me a chance to talk, even if you don't agree. Just knowing that you listen helps me."

# Four

# *Reduce Your Manipulability*

"Don't think that I am going to *forget* this!"

"This is the *last straw!*"

Sound familiar? Statements like these are often made by adult children whose parents have found just the right emotional buttons to push—and have pushed them.

A son once told me how he had decided to take his father to a "great" (his father said, "expensive") restaurant for a birthday celebration. The choice of restaurant highlighted the differences between the two men.

A second-generation Polish-American, steelworker, and union man, the father shopped at K-Mart, J.C. Penney, and no-name discount stores. For him, a night out was at Captain D's or some other fast-food shop.

The son was a college-educated lawyer and popular after-dinner speaker. He shopped at Brooks Brothers and Saks, and wore only Hart, Schafner, and Marx suits—top of the line. For *him,* a night out was most likely in one of the city's fanciest restaurants.

The son's generation had been the first to go to college, and he had hustled to get through. He graduated with an academic record good enough to get him fellowships in an MBA program and then law school.

He had married well ("too well," said his father; "She's 'highfalutin,' " was his mother's comment). His wife was from one of Chicago's best suburbs. He wanted it all, and she was part of the package.

Her family connections had opened the right doors for him. But en route she had given up on her pesky father-in-law. "A peasant, truly," she said. She begged off the birthday dinner, saying she had a headache.

"Where's Ruthie?" his father asked when he got in the car. (He had often been corrected: "My name is *Ruth!*")

"Headache." That one word, together with the brief look exchanged, was enough explanation.

"Oh. Where we gonna eat, Mr. Bigshot Attorney? I'm starved."

"It's a surprise. . . ."

Thirty minutes later, they sat in the City Club, the 32nd floor, overlooking the city. At their table the father found matches with his name embossed in gold on the cover.

"Pretty highfalutin place, as your mother would say."

"No place is too good for my dad on his birthday!"

The evening went better than the son had anticipated. But it all unraveled when the waiter recognized the son.

"Aren't you . . .? I've read about you in the papers."

"Yeah," the father interrupted. "I could tell you a thing or two about this guy." The waiter's surprised look encouraged him. "Third grade he went to Brandeis Elementary School. A shy little punk. Too shy to ask to go to the toilet." The word sounded out of place in the City Club.

"Dad?"

"Shhhh. I'm talking now. So he poops in his pants . . . ," his father laughed, "right there. The teacher asked about it and he lied." (By now the son had turned four shades of crimson.) "And he had to ride home on the school bus . . . stinking." The father held his nose to emphasize the point.

The lawyer-son sunk his teeth into his lips, fighting back his anger.

"Yeah. Pooped 'em!" The father's cackling laughter underscored the insult.

"The check, please," the son growled.

"Hey, sonny boy, I ain't had dessert yet. The old man ought to be entitled to some cake on his birthday!"

They rode home: the son silently rumbling like a volcano, the father chattering away. "Night, boy," he said as he got out of the car.

*"Happy birthday, Dad!"* the son snapped back with barely restrained anger.

There were no thank-yous. The son drove for an hour— screaming, crying, raging. His dad could get under his skin the way no attorney or judge or jury in the city of Chicago could do.

## Familiar themes

As this attorney told me his story, I recognized some familiar themes and ingredients. Many people could tell similar stories. If you changed a detail here and there, the story could be mine or yours.

I asked this son if he had ever talked to his father about the incident.

"You *can't* talk to him!" he responded. "About anything! I've never been able to talk to him."

A well-known evangelistic leader told me he nearly slugged

his father after a similar encounter at a family gathering. I think of a woman named Ellen who swore that "never again" would she let herself be humiliated. She hasn't talked to her mother in five years.

Perhaps you, too, recognized something in the attorney's story that recalls an old wound. Perhaps your wounds are not so dramatic, and seem insignificant by comparison. But are your Band-Aids holding?

## *The need for intervention*

Just as there is no such thing as an insignificant cancer cell, so there is no such thing as an insignificant insult. Your grievances against your parents are tumors growing on your emotions. Unless you intervene, and soon, the stakes will grow bigger and so will the consequences.

Some people get diarrhea or colitis just thinking about being with their parents. Many adult children lie in the dark after a family visit, fuming, rehearsing all the "I should have saids."

How many mates have seen their spouses wounded? Have watched them act as if they were unaffected, and then listened to a tirade all the way home? How many have snapped back, "Don't take it out on *me*!"?

Some parents are emotional CPAs. They have a ledger sheet on which they record those, "After all I have done for yous." They may have selective recall about your successes, but they are good at listing your failures:

- "Oh yeah? Well, what about the time you . . . and I . . .?"
- "If it hadn't been for me. . . ."

Some parents are skilled at this, but don't see themselves as manipulators. It's second nature to them. Others are mean-spirited: they intend to wound. Often, it's the fine line between the two that leads to fights between spouses.

"She did it *deliberately!*" a daughter-in-law complains. Now the son is caught between wife and mother.

"Honey, that's just her. You have to ignore her. You can't take it so seriously." That's the son's way of trying to escape. Often he knows differently.

If a husband does not understand that his wedding vows include a vow to forsake mother and father, the problem will intensify.

Some parents want "perfect" occasions: "It won't be the same if you're not here." They subtly use magic words or phrases to manipulate.

What about Christmas, that great family time of the year? If you really had your choice, how would you spend Christmas? Would you drive 350 miles to see your folks or to be with your mate's parents? Sleep on a couch? Share a bathroom? Would you?

Some friends of mine once made a decision to spend their first Christmas as husband and wife in Nashville rather than go to be with either set of parents. Stunned, I quizzed them about their reasons.

"It's the way to start our own tradition and avoid a fight," they said. For some couples, however, such a decision would only result in *two* sets of angry parents.

It's one thing to recognize the fact that you are being manipulated, and it's another to fume the whole time. Sometimes adult children have the attitude of a child made to sit in the corner, who snaps, "I may be sitting down on the *outside,* but on the *inside* I'm standing up!" There are a lot of 42-year-olds, 52-year-olds, and 62-year-olds who say the same thing.

It may be that you get manipulated into spending every Fourth of July with your parents and the clan, or an entire week of your vacation. How many family occasions have been spoiled by repressed anger or annoyance?

## *Guidelines to help you resist manipulation*

If you don't want to be manipulated, then don't be. If you *are* manipulated, try to make the best of it. Bill made the decision not to go home for Christmas—but he also made airline reservations in case he caved in.

*1. Practice diffusing the code words.*    Some older parents (who are more skilled, one man argued) use emotion-laden, coded language, like, "This could be our last Christmas together. . . ." With the right tone of voice and pauses, these statements can be very effective. There is a degree of truth to it: it could in fact be your last Christmas together. But that is also true of any Christmas—at any age.

What phrases work the best on you? Repeat them now. Aloud. Again. Can you imitate the tone? Now, explain the motivation that lies behind the phrase.

What are your responses to these phrases going to be? Say them out loud. Put in an exclamation mark or two for emphasis.

Some people have found it helpful to role-play. Get a friend to play your parent's part (encourage them to be good at it). With their help, create the conversation that you expect to take place. Make it as realistic as possible. The first time you try it, it may be difficult or you may feel dumb, but remember: this kind of an exercise will be one more snip in that unhealthy umbilical cord that entangles you.

*2. Pray about it.*    If you have decided that *no* is the right answer, ask God to help you be gentle but firm. This also reduces damage to such things as telephones. Too many of them get broken by being slammed down after a talk with parents.

*3. Reinforce your decision.*    Say something like, "You know, mom, I can understand why you would like me (or us) to do that, but this is not the year. I have to think of what is best for everyone."

## *Breaking the manipulation habit*

In 1 Samuel 20, Saul railed at Jonathan, "You son of a perverse and rebellious woman! Don't I know that you have sided with the son of Jesse to your own shame and the shame of the mother who bore you?" (v. 30). Saul knew what Jonathan's emotional threshold was, and he went for the jugular. From the social context of 1 Samuel we can tell that Saul was accusing Jonathan of being homosexually involved with David. There was no proof to the charge, but Jonathan's love for David was real, and his father had struck a vulnerable nerve.

We do not know much about Jonathan's mother—she might have *been* perverse and rebellious. But more likely Saul was using a Hebrew equivalent to the crude English expression, "You S.O.B.!" The point is, Saul wanted to annoy Jonathan. And by using this double insult, he succeeded:

> Jonathan got up from the table in fierce anger; that second day of the month he did not eat, because he was grieved at his father's shameful treatment of David (v. 34).

Jonathan had a good reason to leave the table—his father had thrown his spear at him. Too often, though, adult children leave the table or the room without responding to their parents' verbal manipulation. One of the benefits of a role-playing exercise is that you won't be taken by surprise. You anticipate what your parents will say and your own reactions to that. That's why football teams look at the films of their opponents. They don't want to make a big mistake or be surprised.

Suppose you've always given in. Your parent now assumes that you will give in this time, too. If you had dealt with the pattern of manipulation six months ago (or six years ago), you wouldn't be facing the problem now. Being manipulated is a habit—a bad habit. But no one can manipulate you without some degree of assistance on your part.

The pattern of manipulation *can* be broken.

Maybe you want to tell me about those times you have given in when "everything worked out fine." Congratulations. It may have worked out in part because you chose not to harbor feelings of resentment about being manipulated. You made the second, but equally important, choice—*to make the best of it.*

In some families, resisting manipulation takes a joint effort. One son or daughter may not be able to do it. But two or three can.

Suppose your brother makes a decision not to come home for Christmas this year and sticks with that decision. How will you respond?

● *Maybe you will need to defend him.* In some families there will be those, "If only Joe was here" comments just as you open presents or sit down to dinner. In other families it will be harsher: "I don't understand why he couldn't be here!" You may need to say, "Mom, Joe is an adult. I'm sure he had good reasons. . . ." Be sure to smile a lot during such exchanges.

● *Ponder involvement in second-wave manipulation.* Suppose your mother enlists your help: "Call Joe and talk to him. He'll listen to you . . . ," or, "Maybe you can get him to change his mind." It's true, these requests are hard to resist, because you know how much it means to your parents. But second-wave manipulation often comes across as angry or accusing: "Joe, why don't you think of someone besides yourself?"

Perhaps you agree to call him, but later say that you forgot. Or you might have remembered to call, but it happened to be at a time when you knew that Joe wasn't home.

There might be a family occasion that is important enough to merit a tag-team effort, but few of them are.

● *Anticipate the full assault.* Many parents will not stop until they get a yes for an answer. I once saw a sign that said, "Salesmanship does not begin until the customer says, 'No.' "

The same is true of manipulation. Some parents have developed a system of escalating pressures until they finally bring in the heavy artillery:

1. request
2. annoyance
3. silence
4. brooding
5. "Wear 'em down."

Parents use:

1. *words*
2. *silences*
3. *bribes*—"I have already bought you a present, but it's too fragile to mail."
4. *rewards*—after the yes is gained, you get an adult lollipop. It takes a strong person to resist.

I think of Ed and Millie, who live in Tulsa. Three of their adult children are married and live in Kansas City. Every time Ed and Millie plan to visit their children, grandma (Ed's mother) gets sick. The pattern begins midweek; by late Thursday night, the "death rattles" are there. On Monday morning she reports, "I nearly died. . . ."

While Ed and Millie have a responsibility to his mother, they also have a responsibility to themselves to get away for breathers and to see their children and grandchildren. His mother's control almost became divisive between them, until Millie put her foot down: "We're going to Kansas City!"

Finally, they told his mother:

"Here's the phone number where we will be."

"You're welcome to go with us. . . ."

"We can be back in a few hours if you really need us."

That firmness is paying off. Now Ed can finally relax and enjoy the visits (the first one made him a nervous wreck: "How will I feel if she should die while I'm up here?"). He has also stopped buying trinkets to placate her: "See, mother, I brought you something. . . ."

The experience caused Ed and Millie to say to each of their children, "Don't let us manipulate you. If we start, just say, "Mom (or Dad), you're acting just like grandma!"

Patterns of manipulation are easy to get into and difficult to break. But it is possible to change them. Instead of resigning yourself to the situation and feeling like you are a victim, you can choose to improve your relationship.

Here are four things to remember that will help you break the cycle of manipulation.

1. Your parents know what buttons to push to get a rise out of you. They have had years to watch you. They have "selective recall" of those experiences you hope they have forgotten.

2. Sometimes you must simply "grin and bear it." It's no fun to be on the receiving end of a taunt, regardless of how harmless it is supposed to be, and the best you can do is diffuse the wallop by ignoring it.

3. Always consider the option of not responding. Be unpredictable. As long as your parents know that pushing certain buttons will get a reaction out of you, they will be able to manipulate you. By choosing not to respond, you break the cycle and regain control of your own responses. And remember: your goal is not to turn the game around and start manipulating your *parents*. Instead, work toward establishing a new and better way of relating to one another.

4. Anticipate the guilt-producing line, "After all I've done for you. . . ." Create some responses of your own to counter with, like, "What? Didn't you get that thank-you note I sent you for all you've done?" or, "I appreciate all you've done. I know that you've sacrificed for me, but I had hoped that you would understand. . . ."

Remember, change doesn't come overnight. Manipulative techniques are habit-forming. But if you think, plan, and pray ahead of time, you can reduce and diffuse their impact and their power over you.

*Five*

# Resist Your Parents' Curiosity

Curiosity killed the cat! It has also maimed, and even destroyed, relationships between many adult sons and daughters and their parents.

"My mother missed her calling in life," said one 30-year-old doctor. "She should have been a district attorney. She has more questions than a new convert."

A mother of three noted, "She calls at 10:00 P.M., 'Just checking to see how everything is.' I know she's fishing for something."

I laughed with the woman who said, "My mother's vocabulary consists of six words: *who, what, when, where, how,* and *why.* Especially *why!*"

## Old habits are hard to break

Some parents have an insatiable curiosity. Nothing is too trivial, too mundane: your two-year-old's bowel habits, your choice of laundry powder, your 14-year-old's dating habits, how much you spent on food last week. . . .

One mother defended herself by saying, "How am I going to find out if I don't ask?"

Remember, for many years—almost two decades—your parents' lives and even their conversations focused on you. Changing those habits is very difficult.

In fact, researchers have found that for many husbands and wives, their children are the *chief* subjects of conversation. "What should we do about Little League? About the youth group? About college?"

Some couples look up one day and suddenly discover that they have little to talk about anymore. That's the danger of childcentric marriages.

Parents' curiosity about the lives of their adult children is also stimulated by boredom. Are your parents active with other people their age? Do they read? Travel? Are they joiners? Do they both work? The more stimulating interests that they have, the less time they will have to be curious about yours. But if their chief preoccupation is with the TV, it should not be surprising that they are curious; their brains are fighting for survival: "I think I'll pick up the phone and call Mary. . . . "

I sometimes wonder if, after the big reunion dinner for the prodigal son (Luke 15), his dad said, "Now tell me all about it! What was it like?"

The older your parents are, the more likely they are to brag about you. So they are always in need of new data, "the latest." With the upward mobility available to many of us today, we sometimes live out things that our parents only fantasized about. In one recent week, my speaking schedule took me to Mexico, the Grand Cayman Islands, and Jamaica. Naturally, my parents are curious. My mother has been in maybe 10 states in her life. She's flown in an airplane once.

The intense curiosity of many parents contrasts sharply with the indifference of others, who don't particularly care to see your pictures from Rome, Georgia or Rome, Italy, or those parents who resent the fun you are having.

Curiosity is also stimulated by distance. In the days when it was common for several generations of one family to live in the same town, parents didn't have to ask. Everybody knew. A complex network of social relationships supplied the data. "I saw your son's new car," a neighbor would say. The party line telephone was a treasury of local gossip.

The media, too, have played a role in fostering curiosity. George Gallup and other pollsters are always telling us that 67.7% of Americans believe $x$, $y$, and $z$, or that 57.3% *do x*, *y*, and *z*. So your parents may decide to conduct their own poll.

You may be a single woman, living alone, and an article reports that 77.6% of single women, living alone, are sexually active. Something triggers your mother's curiosity when she reads that. Initially, she may wonder but not ask. But the longer she goes without asking, the more anxious she becomes.

However, she may not risk asking you directly. So she constructs a carefully-phrased question. She may say, "Did you see that article in _____ ?" as an attempt to prime the pump.

"Yeah," you respond, without enthusiasm. Some parents immediately place an answer like that under the microscope. It's even worse if you try to change the subject.

Rarely will parents ask you if you are in the 77.6% that do or the 22.4% that do not. They hope you will give them enough data to relieve their anxiety.

## *The positive side of curiosity*

One of the reasons parents today ask their adult children so many questions is that they are having to deal with issues and life-styles that *their* parents could hardly have imagined.

Questions—even the tough ones—sometimes help to keep the airwaves clear. They can be like a sudden thunderstorm on a hot, summer night. An absence of curiosity can lead to misunderstanding and unnecessary worry.

If you take off your mom or dad's head every time they ask a question, to some degree you heighten their fear. They will still worry, but they will be afraid to ask.

One mother and her grown daughter worked out the following arrangement: the mother is free to ask anything—no topic is off-limits; the daughter is equally free not to answer.

Witnesses before congressional committees often plead their Fifth Amendment privilege: "I choose not to answer on the grounds that it may incriminate me." Every citizen has this right; not every parent, however, will grant the same right to an adult child.

One of the disadvantages of taking the Fifth, either before Congress or in front of your parents, is that people tend to ask, "What have you got to hide?" By this point in our lives, most of us have a number of things we would rather not have brought out in the open. There are some choices, decisions, sins, mistakes, and business deals that we don't want our parents to know about. That's one of the reasons marriage conflicts and divorce proceedings can get so nasty—one spouse may decide to "rat" on their mate to an in-law.

We may say, "My life's an open book," but is it really? Some of us have worked hard to live up to our parents' expectations, to be the "blessings" they wanted us to be. We have behaved ourselves, become achievers—and kept our closets tightly locked. Usually there are some things that we just don't want them to know about.

## Parental investigations

In 1984, when I decided to go to Yugoslavia and Turkey, I decided not to tell my parents until the day I left. My parents are worriers. My mother told me, "I wish you weren't going!"

For the same reason, I do not share information about my finances with my parents. My mom and dad have a small house, with two bedrooms, one bath, and 900 square feet. They paid $80 a month for 20 years, and it's theirs. I've never told them what my mortgage payments are—they would die! But that's part of the reality of home ownership today.

However, if I had taken a trinket from them (see Chapter 7), like a down payment, I would be somewhat obligated to share more data with them. And that could lead to a subjective evaluation: "That's an awful lot to pay for a house," or a judgment: "I wouldn't if I were you!"

But when data is kept from parents, there may be problems later on. If disaster should strike and they become aware of it, they will naturally ask, "How long has this been going on?" Most parents will be offended that you kept important information from them.

Some parents have learned to enlist grandchildren in their intelligence-gathering network. Children do not always understand the nuances of the questions they are asked or know how to filter information. So they will tell you "about the time mommy. . . ."

Some parents are skilled at playing the district attorney. Just like on TV, they know how to drill a witness with rapid-fire questions, one after the other. They may even badger the witness. They structure a question and then demand a yes or a no. The witness hesitates, and then comes more pressure: "Yes or no!"

But some questions are hard to answer with a simple yes or no, like the old line, "Do you still beat your wife?" A *no* implies that you once did beat your wife. You're trapped.

Some parents make a good interrogation team. They switch off with each other: "See if you can get it out of 'em!" Or they compare answers: "What did he tell *you?*"

Admittedly, your parents do not put you under oath: "I do solemnly swear to tell the truth, the whole truth, and nothing but the truth." Yet the prospect of not telling the truth to your parents brings back all those childhood memories. For some of us, the most severe punishments we received from our parents were for times when we lied to them.

We know that lying is wrong. But there is always that gray area that we wrestle with. Haven't you felt that twinge of guilt that comes when you mislead your parents, when you set them up to draw a certain conclusion, or when you put out a smoke screen to prevent them from following your actions too closely?

Some of us really have been guilty of misleading our parents. In other cases, though, we merely *feel* guilty, and all we have actually done is chosen not to tell them the whole truth.

## Ten basic guidelines

The problem is clear. But what can we do about it? Here are some guidelines that should help:

*1. Anticipate your parents' curiosity.* By anticipating, you avoid feeling like you have been put on the spot. Your parents will generally follow predictable patterns with you. Identify them and prepare for them. For example, if your dad says, "Let's go for a walk or a drive," you may know that something's up.

*2. Rehearse your answers.* You have anticipated what they will ask you. Now actually rehearse your responses. Stand in front of a mirror. Stand straight. Look them in the eye. Say out loud what you're going to say to them.

Rehearsing your answers is important, because otherwise you will have a tendency to say, *"Mother!"* or "That's none of your business!'' You are more likely to be in control and remain in control.

*3. Diffuse the question.* ''Why do you want to know?'' They might have a good and reasonable answer.

*4. Limit or deny the information.* ''I can understand, mother, why you would ask. I hope you can understand why I don't want to discuss this.''

*5. Change the subject.*

*6. Take a time-out.* Go to the bathroom. Get a drink of water. Take a walk. Your parent may conclude that you are stalling, but that's OK. At least you stay in control of your responses.

*7. Don't be coerced.* Some children have been pressured— against their better judgment—into talking. Many have then regretted it, because it fueled the notion that, ''My mother won, again. I am always a child with her.''

*8. Recognize the question for what it may be: a test of power.* Ask yourself, ''Who's in control?'' Remind yourself that you are no longer a child, but an adult son or daughter.

*9. Don't drag in the past.* Some people who get hysterical get historical: ''You always do this to me!'' Don't let the past become present-tense.

*10. If appropriate, give them a time when you will talk about it.*

However, there is another option that you may find necessary: *to revoke the privilege.* One of my counselees had two grandchildren who were living with their mother (her daughter-in-law). More data: the daughter-in-law was living with a man.

So every time the children came to grandmother, she asked lots of questions.

The two grandchildren had been warned and even punished by their mother for talking too much. But the grandmother offered them candy, clothes, money, and promises. She was seeking "the slip" that could reopen the custody case.

The result is that two precious children are caught in the cross fire. My advice to the grandmother was, "Knock it off!"

As an adult son or daughter, you have the privilege of terminating a conversation. You don't have to slam down the telephone receiver. You can say, "Mother (or Father), I have to go now. Good-bye." That's tough to do, but it's extremely helpful. How many adult children fume for 30 minutes after talking to a parent because they let the conversation go on and on, or drift into areas that they don't want to talk about?

Some parents will ignore your gentle warning signals. Sometimes we adults have to be assertive.

Ask yourself four questions:

1. Will it help?
2. Is it true?
3. Will I feel the same way tomorrow?
4. Does it implicate others or complicate their choices or relationships with other siblings?

## *Saul and Jonathan*

In 1 Samuel 20:27, Saul demanded to know from Jonathan, "Why hasn't the son of Jesse come to the meal, either yesterday or today?" The simple answer would have been that it's hard to eat and enjoy the meal (to say nothing of the effect on digestion) when you are dodging spears thrown by the host.

Jonathan lied. Oh, he probably didn't consider it a lie. He couldn't say, "Because you are trying to kill him!" so instead he answered,

David earnestly asked me for permission to go to Bethlehem. He said, "Let me go, because our family is observing a sacrifice in the town and my brother has ordered me to be there. If I have found favor in your eyes, let me get away to see my brothers." That is why he has not come to the king's table (vv. 28-29).

But Saul wasn't buying it. He exploded. "You son of a perverse and rebellious woman! Don't I know that you have sided with the son of Jesse to your own shame and to the shame of the mother who bore you?" (v. 30). I have a feeling that at this point the other diners put their forks down. "No dessert to-night," they probably concluded. Sometimes any answer you give is going to be the wrong one. And the breach between Saul and Jonathan was now complete.

## The abuse of curiosity

Sometimes a parent's right to "cross-examine" must be re-voked. A lot of people don't go home as often and don't phone as often because curiosity has been abused. Or perhaps the material that was shared was used to hurt someone else.

Some parents play one sibling off against another. After a while, the "You said/he saids" get complicated. You may be resistant to your parents' curiosity, but what about your brother or sister? A parent may be able to get the data through them. Suppose you share something personal with a brother. Are you sure it won't get back to mom and dad?

Suppose you tell your brother, George, that you don't want to come home for Christmas. Then your mother calls and says, "I hear that you don't want to come home for Christmas."

If you do find it necessary to revoke the privilege, it is good to provide documentation: "Mom, let me remind you about the time I told you something, and you went and told George.

. . ." Dates, places, and specific wounds that were inflicted may help them understand your decision.

## *Understanding your parents' perspective*

In a few years you will be older. You may have grown children yourself. Then you will see from another perspective. It is natural for parents to have a deep concern for their children and for their welfare, even when they have "left the nest" and are on their own. Mothers are particularly likely to worry about their grown children—partly because of the amount of time that they have traditionally invested in them. In her book *And You Thought It Was All Over,* Zenith Gross quoted one mother of several adult children, who reflected a common attitude: "No mother is happier than her *least* happy child." Another mother said, "I can't put my head down peacefully on the pillow at night if something is not quite right with one of them—I feel a sort of unease."[1]

In ancient Israel, a shepherd was expected to know the condition of the flocks (Prov. 27:23). As they help their children learn and grow, parents take at least as much concern over them as a shepherd does over the sheep. Most parents feel the need to know how you are. They want to be reassured. The ones who brought you into the world, who nursed and cared for you when you were helpless, who know your history of fears, also know that there are adult equivalents of boogeymen and bad dreams and tricycle falls.

When does concern turn into curiosity? Is there a chalk line that a parent steps over that offends his or her children?

Too many adult sons or daughters have overreacted to their parents' curiosity and posted "No Trespassing" signs. There is much that parents and children can share without succumbing to the curiosity game. And perhaps the greatest challenge is to learn not only how and when to limit the sharing of information, but also how to increase the sharing of feelings that lie behind the information.

Dealing with parental curiosity is not something that you do once and for all. It is one of the items on your adult agenda that you must work at over and over. If your parents are interested enough in your lives to ask, be thankful for that. But work toward a way of answering their questions that respects both your independence and your relationship with them.

# Six

# *Regulate Your Time Together*

"Is it mothering or smothering?" Sometimes it is hard to know. There was something picturesque about all the Waltons comfortably ensconced under the old Virginia farmhouse roof, calling out, "Goodnight, John Boy . . .," as we softly hummed "Home on the Range." If only more families could honestly say, "Where never is heard a discouraging word."

## *Changing family patterns*

Historically, couples often started their married lives under the roof of one set of parents, because there was a housing shortage and a need to build up a nest egg. Yet as Archie Bunker discovered, that made for confusion and frustration. "Who's in charge here, anyway?"

My mom and dad lived with my dad's parents during their first year of marriage. That is, they lived with his parents, his older sister and her husband, 10 other children, and a few farmhands. Next they moved to a small cottage on my grandfather's farm. For the first six years of my life I slept in the living room or dining room on a roll-away bed because my sister, her husband, and their two children lived with us. Families did those things.

Perhaps your grandparents lived with you at some point. This often happened before the government got into subsidizing high-rise senior adult residences. In many families it would have been unthinkable to have put grandmother or grandfather into any type of care center. My mom struggled with breaking that tradition. I recall my step-grandmother saying, "Couldn't you make a place for him?" My mother already had two kids at home and three active grandchildren. There was no place for grandad—especially with his personality and medical difficulties.

Perhaps you come from one of those families that try to be together as much as they possibly can. Are you expected for Sunday dinner? Is every holiday predetermined? The old pattern of physically living together under one roof may not be true for you (although it is becoming more and more common again), but your family may have strong traditions about being together, and that can create similar problems.

Since World War II another new wrinkle has emerged in parent-child relationships: the parent as pal or buddy. Some parents try to develop a "best friends" relationship with their children.

I contend that parents are not designed to be pals, friends, or buddies. Rejection of their traditional role has led to a confusion of authority. Child psychologists are alarmed by the new, egalitarian families. A power vacuum is created, and children are known to stage coups. Each successful coup only makes the stakes larger. These are situations where someone *should* ask, "Who's in charge here?"

Today, many of us are caught in the cross fire as traditional values and transitional values fight for dominance. We are trying to find workable patterns for our relationships, and we are strongly influenced by our inner feelings about the way "things are supposed to be."

## *The need for regulation*

Adult sons and daughters need to regulate their time with their parents. If you say, "Oh, but we do everything together," then there is good reason to believe you have a problem. Adults need their own peer social patterns that correspond with the needs of their own particular stage in life.

Familiarity really *can* breed contempt. For example, how do you discipline your children in front of their grandparents? Does it become obvious that the child has the upper hand? Do your parents ever veto your disciplinary measures, or sabotage their effectiveness? You may end up giving in, and then the child receives conflicting signals from you.

Too much time spent together also blocks the formation of other beneficial relationships, both for you and your parents. This often happens when grown children assume custody of their parents. Soon their own social patterns are altered. Joan said, "I wouldn't mind taking my mother out to dinner, but you can't find a restaurant that will please her. It's impossible. I've tried. She'd find something to gripe about if she were eating at the White House!"

Joan's mother counters by saying, "Ellie (her friend) goes out to eat with *her* daughter!"

The problem can become acute if you decide to have one or both of your parents come live with you. One daughter complained, "She is always there to criticize me. 'I think you should do it this way. . . .' She starts at 7:00 A.M., and is still at it at midnight!"

It's important to balance a sense of responsibility with firmness. Parents should already have a niche in your heart, but some will insist on much more than that. They will want sovereignty. And as an adult son or daughter, that is something you cannot give, especially if you have made a marriage vow to "forsake all others."

Singles can be placed under particular pressure. American tradition suggests that an unmarried daughter should either remain at home with her parents, or at least be more responsible for their welfare. Some daughters have seen numerous opportunities for marriage disappear because of this. If you choose to give in to this tradition, you should be forewarned that it can breed resentment. The system tends to be reinforced by married brothers or sisters, because it reduces their responsibility. "After all," they can argue, "we have families of our own."

There are understandable reasons why parents look forward to spending time with their children. Let's face it, when many people are placed in senior residences, they become bored. There just isn't that much to do, and they may or may not find others their age whom they enjoy being with. *Your* family life—whatever it is like—provides familiarity, a sense of belonging, and a change of pace.

Where the problem comes in, however, is when a parent insists, "I'm *still* your father (or mother)."

Some mates get tired of dropping in on their in-laws. They choose to remain in their car or snap, "Make it quick."

For single adults with limited social lives, it's easy to return to the comfort and security of mom and dad's couch at the first sign of loneliness or fear. Many single adults have never given living on their own a fair chance.

## Eight basic guidelines

Here are eight guidelines that can help you responsibly regulate the time you spend with your parents.

*1. Determine how much time you will spend.* You may intend to stick your head in and get a quick summary of how they are. They want you to sit and stay a while. "What's your hurry?" You need to have decided in advance exactly how long you will stay.

*2. Ignore the bait.* "*Harvey's* not too busy to come see his mother!" Well, Harvey may still be tied to his mother's apron strings. Or he may be battling with his wife every time he comes. Or Harvey's mother may work hard to make the visits as pleasant as possible. Simply let Harvey be Harvey.

Other common forms of bait are:

● "Someday *you'll* be old. . . ."

● "When I'm gone, you'll wish you'd had time for your poor, old mother. . . ."

Such phrases and heart-tugs have the ability to reduce a CPA or Ph.D. to emotional mush.

If you have decided beforehand how long you can stay, then you will not have to make excuses about why you can't stay any longer than that.

*3. Expect the worst.* Change comes slowly. Some sons and daughters think, *This time things will be different.* Then they feel disappointed when tradition wins again. Unrealistic expectations have the effect of leaving everyone disappointed. Not all families can have reunions that remind you of the Waltons.

*4. Determine your countermoves.* Your parents may be of the school that children—even adult children—are to be seen and not heard. They may insist on doing most of the talking. So what do you do when they start rehearsing all of their ailments? Do you nod? Do you listen with one ear? Sneak glances at your watch? Try to change the subject?

Sometimes it is wise to have previously rehearsed questions

that you can ask them—questions that are not necessarily open-ended.

Another helpful countermove is a "time-out" or bathroom break. Asking, "Would you like to go for a walk?" can be a way of getting out of a sticky situation.

You may wish to gently question the accuracy of your parents' statements of gloom and doom. "Oh, mother, I don't think you look bad. Your color is good." Be positive. You don't have to come home from every visit with parents with a case of the blues. Take the initiative in setting the tone for your time together.

*5. Don't let yourself be manipulated.*    In chapter 19 of the book of Judges, a parent's "Oh, please stay!" led to disastrous consequences. When a Levite arrived at his father-in-law's house, he was talked into staying for three days. On the fourth day, the son-in-law "got up early and he prepared to leave" (v. 5), but the father-in-law prevailed. The next day, the son-in-law left, "unwilling to stay another night" (v. 10). I can just imagine him, mumbling to himself, as he headed toward Jerusalem.

Sometimes cranky kids offer parents a perfect exit line: "We've got to go so we can get these kids to bed." But it's hard for adult children to find an equally convincing line to use with their parents.

Remember, you are an adult. If you are manipulated by your parents, it is because you allow yourself to be.

*6. Push for ground rules for a visit.*    One son wrote to his parents, saying, "Just once I'd like to come home and not fuss or fight." Alex Haley, author of *Roots,* observed, "We never have a reunion without a fight breaking out. . . . but we keep having them anyway, because reunions bring out how much we care for each other. We patch our rifts, and in the end, the joys outbalance anything else that happens.''[1] Not everyone would come to the same conclusion as Haley did. Many have vowed, "Never again," only to cave in six months or a year later. It is especially difficult to discount or contradict the statement, "It won't be the same without you."

I wish there had been some ground rules in effect when my grandmother came to visit. She belonged to a religious group that said, in effect, "If you don't believe it and do it exactly the way we do, you ain't got it." She baited my father every time she visited. I grew to dread it. I remember that she thought television was particularly demonic. She also had strong opinions on hemlines, makeup, and jewelry, among other things. *Many* other things.

The visits frustrated me because I couldn't stand her attempts to influence my father. Yet other kids in the neighborhood told me that it was supposed to be fun when grandma visited.

I did notice that when we visited *her*—for brief periods of time—my father went on automatic pilot. He answered her questions, but that was about it. "Good time to get the car washed. . . . "

*7. Regulate your telephone contact.*   One man was confused by his wife's reaction to her in-laws. "Why should she object to me calling my parents?" he asked.

"Six or seven times a day?" she countered.

Some parents are skillful phone technicians. They say things over the phone that they would not say in person. Maybe Mr. Bell's invention has not been as helpful as many have thought. Zenith Gross says,

One of the most enduring visual images of the mature family is a picture of Mom on the telephone with one or another of the adult children for many long minutes (even hours), while Dad dances agitatedly in the background, pointing to his watch, miming a cash register, or just shrugging his shoulders in annoyance.[2]

Furthermore, families of very modest means, who once perceived long-distance phone calls as being only for extreme emergencies, have come to accept the expense as a necessary price of keeping the family connected. In one study of 500 mothers, nearly 80% reported that the telephone was the primary channel of contact with their children.[3]

Sometimes I wonder if the message shouldn't be, "It's 10:00 P.M. Do you know *how* your children are?" After all, the phone gives parents who have overactive imaginations a chance to do a quick check on their children. AT&T knows how to generate phone usage with a campaign to "Reach out and touch someone." What this translates into is, "Pick up the phone and call now, or you'll feel guilty!"

Phone companies come out ahead, even when their transmission lines are used to engage in knock-down-drag-out fights at long distance rates.

A telephone exchange can leave both mother and adult son or daughter in a heart-aching misunderstanding that can be repaired only by many additional phone calls or a face-to-face visit or searching letter. Sometimes the misunderstanding cannot be repaired at all, and simmers for a long time, telephone or no, just as it used to be in pre-electronic times—but there are some modern differences.[4]

Where parents once said, "It's good to see you," now the greeting is often, "It's good to hear your voice." Some parents sense that it is a sign of maturity when their son or daughter no longer calls collect.

There may be a need to regulate time with one parent at the expense of another. In American society, it is traditional for the mother to do the calling. And in many families, there is one parent whom the children prefer to talk to in a crisis. Often a mother is the one children call, with news or requests (particularly requests for money) to be passed on to dad. Fathers have learned to listen with the "third ear" via their wives' words. In fact, Lillian Troll contends, "many men count on their wives to keep them in touch with their children and their parents and the loss of a wife can almost sever family communications for older men."[5]

One of your parents will most likely survive the other. You need to be establishing communication links with *both*.

*8. Regulate by issue.*     Some issues, in the interest of family harmony, should be declared off-limits. If my mother's family could have put religion and politics off-limits, we might have had many better memories. When my uncle converted to Catholicism (which incensed my grandmother), it meant that his children saw her less. She could not discipline her anti-Catholic rhetoric.

A newly single man named Bill quipped, "You know the one thing that I haven't missed from my divorce is my in-laws. They were so judgmental. Doctrinally we agreed, but on lifestyles they could not accept us. For example, they came to visit us, so we thought we could go out for a great Sunday brunch. That way Kathy, my wife, wouldn't have to spend hours in the kitchen. But they wouldn't go. It's against their religion to eat out on Sunday. So Kathy slaved away most of the morning on a meal. But I got to thinking—what would they do if they were traveling on Sunday? I asked my father-in-law and he said, 'that would be different.' I never could understand their logic.

"Well, we decided we ought to take them out. We pull up in front of one of the nice restaurants where I had made reservations, and he says, 'Do they serve alcohol in there?' For our anniversary, because he wouldn't go in, we ended up 'celebrating' at Bob's Big Boy."

Other adult sons and daughters talk about how they worry

about saying "the wrong thing" around their parents, so that table conversation becomes strained.

Another area where you may find you need to discipline yourself is memories. Some people have a backlog of bad memories, which have a way of jumping out at the worst possible times.

You may have to decide not to cling to a particular memory. ("I am not going to dwell on that.") Others choose to run the memory in slow-motion, which compounds the pain, as every insult is dissected and relived. John Trent reports,

> Researchers performed an interesting study several years ago, in which they sought to understand how the brain stores memories of past events. Through electrical stimulation, these researchers activated certain areas of the brain which they thought might "hold" memories. To the researchers' delight, many experimental subjects recalled memories with striking clarity, even if the events had occurred years earlier.

> As the experiment progressed, however, an unexpected side effect developed. The subjects not only *recalled* a particular event, but experienced some of the *feelings* associated with that memory as well. For example, if the memory was of an emotionally painful experience, the subject actually reexperienced its pain.[6]

No wonder the apostle Paul encouraged us to think about "whatever is true, whatever is noble, whatever is right, whatever is pure, whatever is lovely, whatever is admirable . . ." (Phil. 4:8). Instead of dwelling on the negative memories, we can choose to think about the more positive ones and create new ones.

## *Jonathan and Saul*

Jonathan had to regulate his time with his father. He realized that he was being baited and manipulated. Jonathan had asked one too many questions: "Why should he [David] be put to death? What has he done?" (1 Sam. 20:32). Saul answered in a unique but unmistakable manner; he "hurled his spear at him to kill him" (v. 33). At last, Jonathan had to face the reality of the situation. All that David had said about his father's intentions was true.

Discussion was no longer possible. So "Jonathan got up from the table in fierce anger; that second day of the month he did not eat, because he was grieved at his father's shameful treatment of David" (v. 34).

Time-outs are important and therapeutic. I don't recommend permanent severing of your ties, but it is often necessary to reduce the amount of time spent together. It may be possible to spend less time, but to make that time a more positive experience for all concerned.

Wanda and Bill called her parents two weeks before Christmas, and they were transparent about their reservations about coming home for Christmas. Although the parents were hurt, they, too, wanted a good time "for all." They agreed to some ground rules. Wanda and Bill cut their stay from the customary week down to three days. Admittedly, they felt awkward at first, but soon they grew more comfortable with each other. "It was the best Christmas in years," Wanda later said. "It meant taking a lot of impromptu walks, but it worked out."

"Absence makes the heart grow fonder" is an old cliché that has a kernel of truth in it. It may be that you are spending too much time with your parents—especially if you are in business together.

Perhaps, by regulating your time together, you will be able to make small improvements. This may be a time for planting the seeds of a new relationship, a time to take some concrete steps toward healing.

# Seven

# Duck the Trinkets

*Trinkets.* Those little things that say, "I love you" but can say far more in the unspoken language of family relationships. Some parents resemble Santa Claus, and in some families, almost any day can be Christmas.

The Roman writer Virgil said, "I fear Greeks even when they bring gifts." Dare we paraphrase him and say, "Beware of *parents* bearing gifts?" No matter how beautiful the wrapping paper is, there are often strings attached to the gift—conditions, expectations.

Webster defines a *bribe* as "a price, reward, gift or favor bestowed or promised with a view to pervert the judgment or corrupt the conduct," or "something that serves to induce or influence to a given line of conduct." Sometimes the line between a bribe and a trinket is a very fine one.

The definition of a *trinket* is "a small article or ornament; a thing of little value." Originally, a trinket was a shoemaker's knife. The word came from the Latin *truncare*—to cut off. That's a little ironic, because a trinket given by a parent doesn't "cut off" at all—it only tightens the parental hold.

For adult sons or daughters, accepting a trinket can be like a boy putting his hand into a jar of jelly beans after being told he can have as many as he wants. As he attempts to retrieve his hand from the small-necked jar, he discovers he can't—his hand is full.

Trinkets or other perks keep many children—regardless of their age—in line. It may be a wrapped gift or it might be a wrapped promise: "Some day, my boy, all this will be yours!"

## *What is a trinket to you?*

Something that may be a trinket or a bribe for you might not be one for someone else. It's somewhat economically relative.

Trinkets can include:
- home-cooked meals ("Drop in anytime.")
- laundry/ironing
- shopping sprees (whether at K-Mart or Saks Fifth Avenue)
- condo or house down payments at reduced or no interest
- loans ("Why borrow from a bank when you don't have to?")
- family vacations
- reaching for the bill at a restaurant
- Christmas excesses
- free baby-sitting
- free yard work/painting/appliance repair

The problem is complicated by grandparent economics. Many of today's grandparents no longer fit the stereotype of spending all their free time reading to their grandchildren, taking walks with them, and talking to them about things like fishing and tractors. Because of distances and attitudes,

> . . . grandparents frequently send money now instead of gifts, and of course, it's sensible—the sizes are too difficult to keep up with long distance. Surprises in clothing are often a disastrous mistake for teens who have their own definite tastes, and it is silly (and a waste of postage) to buy the record album in Arizona

or Pennsylvania when it can be purchased (or exchanged) here.
. . . still . . . something is missing.[1]

Moreover, women's roles have changed. We now have many mothers and grandmothers who are working outside the home. Grandmothers were once expected *to be there* to take care of their grandchildren (either for free, or at least for less than the going market rate). However, some grandmothers are resistant and feisty: "I raised *my* children!" one snapped. "You raise *yours!*"

But the expectation and the tradition die hard. Some grandparents respond with cash or gifts. Today most grandmas are not sitting home baking cookies. They have cash to spend on their grandchildren. "Or loot to buy their affection with," as one mother charged.

Some grandparents do baby-sit with secondary motives in mind. That time alone with their grandchildren provides an opportunity for subtle reindoctrination. In some families there are battles between the values and life-style of the parents and those of their grown children. "It's not worth it to have them baby-sit," some parents have concluded.

### High stakes

As the number of trinkets grows, the stakes keep escalating. Eleanor Roosevelt's struggles with her mother-in-law provide a good example. On Christmas 1904, she and F.D.R. opened a small envelope. Inside they found a piece of stationery on which her mother-in-law had sketched a house she intended to build for the young couple. What could they say but, "Thanks"?

Some time after they had moved into the new house, Franklin found Eleanor crying.

This was not her house, she sobbed. She had not helped plan it, and this wasn't the way she wanted to live. Why hasn't she told him this before, her bewildered husband asked. They had gone over the plans together—why hadn't she spoken up? He told her gently that she was not seeing things as they really were, and quickly left the room.[2]

In fact, Franklin's mother had been disappointed when the couple had not moved in with her after their marriage.

How tempting it is for many of us from middle or low-income families to covet the trinkets that wealthy parents can give to their children. Yet we may not fully appreciate how many strings are attached. Eleanor could look around her home and conclude, "It's all hers." Concerning the house they shared while Franklin was governor of New York, she said, "It never was my home in the sense of having anything to do with the furnishing or running of it."[3]

Eleanor said of her mother-in-law, "You were never quite sure when she would appear, day or night." If the interference had only been between Eleanor and Franklin, it might have been easier to handle. But "Mama" Roosevelt

. . . retained control of many of the purse strings in the family and often used this financial leverage to override disciplinary action against her grandchildren. She made them the recipients of lavish gifts—trips to Europe, horses and cars—the latter sometimes coming after the originals had been wrecked. One of the boys told John Gunther that his grandmother was *"the source of all good things in life when we were little kids, if you knew how to handle her."*

I wonder if *your* children see their grandparents as the Roosevelt sons saw theirs: "the source of all good things in life." If it's not in the budget, ask grandma. Eleanor found that her mother-in-law's gift-giving habits became "intrusive forays" made more annoying by "bland protestations of innocence."

She once penned in her diary, "I am so angry at her . . . that it's all I can do to be decent."[4]

Taking a somewhat subjective look at the Roosevelt children, one has to wonder if this interfering grandmother prompted Eleanor to be more protective and defensive of her children than she might have been otherwise. Did Eleanor respond by depriving them of responsibility? None of them chose to carry on their father's involvement in public affairs.

In some families, a trinket may be preferential treatment, doing things for one child at the expense of the others. In other families, a parent may say, "I won't do for one what I can't do for all." On the surface, that sounds like a fair approach. But it isn't always wise to refuse one child something simply because it cannot be done for every child.

In the late 1880s, a South Carolina sharecropper looked at his 17 children and knew that he could not provide an education for all of them. So he prayed that God would give him wisdom to know which one. He chose Mary. That little girl grew up to be Mary McCloud Bethune, founder and president of Bethune-Cookan College in Daytona Beach, Florida, and an advisor to the president of the United States.[5]

Some parents cannot pay for their children's college educations. Other parents believe their children should pay all or part of those costs themselves. And there are some parents who will help a son go through college, but not a daughter. I know one woman who still holds her parents responsible for her lack of a college education.

When there is the ability to help but help is not given, the result can be anger. Walt is 60 years old, and the oldest of 12 children. He didn't get to go out for sports, because he always had chores to do. And he didn't have a chance to go to college. Now he realizes how much higher he could have risen in his company (and how much more money he could have made) if he had had some college. He resents the opportunities that keep coming to his younger brothers and sisters.

In the Roosevelt family, F.D.R. believed that his sons should be allowed to make their own decisions *and mistakes*. Eleanor explained, "I think this attitude came very largely from the fact that his mother had wanted to direct his every thought and deed and that he had had to fight for independence."[6]

Even in the White House, the first lady had to accommodate a mother-in-law who wanted to be first, if not in public power, then in private. When F.D.R.'s campaign manager quit, Eleanor told him: "Brace yourself for a letter, telling you what she thinks; the old lady does not understand anyone refusing a request from the Roosevelts."[7]

Some parents are not willing to take no for an answer. Be firm: trinket giving may not be discouraged by your first attempt to stop it.

## *Financial trinkets*

Trinkets are often financial in nature. Suppose you go every Sunday to your mother's for dinner. In the course of a year, you're saving big bucks. Or suppose your father reaches for the bill at every restaurant, whether it's McDonald's or The Velvet Turtle. Do you just sit there? Do you put up a mock protest? Do you fight for it?

These situations can become a source of real irritation as children insist, "Give me that!" It is said that there is no such thing as a free lunch. Is that also true for Sunday dinner?

In some families, vacations are major trinkets. Sara Delano Roosevelt decided her son's vacation plans. Who decides yours? Maybe your folks have a mountain cabin or a beach condo. After six weeks of summer humidity, you need to "get away from it all." To rent a cabin for two weeks could be prohibitively expensive.

Ask yourself these questions about spending a vacation with your parents:

- Do you go to be with them because you want to?
- Do you go because it's free or subsidized?
- Do you go because it's demanded or traditional? "We will expect you at the beach/lake/mountains in July." Maybe this year is a time for a change. Will you let yourself be talked out of your first preference for a vacation "for the good of the family"?

Carol is a mother of three. Her mother says, "Why would you think of going anywhere else?" But Carol says, "My husband and I really want to go camping. The kids are finally old enough. I kinda hinted that to my mother, and she started in on a tirade about poison ivy and some child who got mauled by a bear in the Smokey Mountains. Of course, I didn't ask about the sharks off the beach by her condo."

If you do choose to go somewhere else on your vacation, will you have to drive several hundred miles out of the way "to swing by the folks for a few days"?

Suppose you need a down payment for a house or a condo. Do you get the money easily from your parents? Do you have to listen to a lot of advice? Have you ever been talked out of a house because your parents thought it was too expensive? It used to be common for parents to help their children get established. At one time that meant 20 acres, some cattle, and a few blankets and seeds. Now it takes a lot more.

Jim and Bev faced this. His parents were farmers, and because they were poor, they didn't even have indoor plumbing until he was a junior in high school. There were six children in three bedrooms.

Bev grew up in a five-bedroom, three-bath, all-electric house. The two of them met in college and were married. When it came time to buy their first house, her father offered a down payment. That hurt Jim's parents; however, he accepted the money. The house wasn't a fixer-upper, and Jim's parents never felt comfortable visiting them there.

Some parents would have had trouble hiding their wounded pride. However, Jim's mom and dad wisely chose to limit their criticism. "It's your life," they told him.

Don is in business with his father-in-law, who has an opinion on everything. Don noted, "I've owned six houses, and my father-in-law has been against me buying every one of them." How did he deal with it? "I listened to what he had to say and then I did what I thought was best."

## *Borrowing money from parents*

How does one go about borrowing money from parents? It's not the same as the "Can I have the car keys tonight?" routine that we went through in high school. In my own case, I needed help to buy my house. I called and asked, "Would it be possible to borrow . . .?" Some sons and daughters are more blunt: "I need _____ dollars by Friday. Could you send it to me?"

Here are five guidelines for borrowing money from parents:

● *Never borrow money needlessly.* Make friends with your banker first. Besides, it will help your credit record. Many people borrow from their parents because they realize a bank would not loan the money to them.

● *Have it in writing:* the amount, terms, payment schedule, and cancellation privilege. One reason for this is in case of death. Suppose your parents don't keep accurate records; how would the administrator of their estate know you have paid in full? Having the loan agreement in writing also helps to prevent misunderstandings with your siblings. When nothing is written down, or things are kept hidden from other family members, problems can result.

● *Make it family knowledge.* Some fathers have nest-egged a son or daughter's dreams. Maybe your brother is too proud to ask for financial help. But he may not be too proud to criticize you for asking for and taking assistance. It saves a lot of bickering and jealousy if everyone knows the terms of a loan.

● *If it is a loan, say so. If you want a gift, ask for a gift.*

● *Recognize the strings.* With the money may come strings. These may be as thin as dental floss or as tough as parachute cord. Suppose you are going to use the money for home remodeling. Does your father suggest you use "Bill," who did the addition to your folks' home? Will you feel comfortable ignoring that? Sometimes strings can be seen in parents' body language: a tight-lipped smile, a raised eyebrow, a subtle clearing of the throat, or an "I see."[8]

## *The roots of trinket-giving*

The roots of trinket-giving begin early in life: "You'll spoil her (or him)," is a phrase grandparents love to hear. Here are some common responses they give:

● "Nonsense," (denial).

● "Oh, really now, it's just a . . ." (slight admittance).

● "Yes, but I'd rather give it now than after I've gone" (appeal to nobility).

How will you respond to those?

As Americans have become more prosperous, there has been an unfortunate tendency within families to substitute gifts for words. Gifts are supposed to mean, "I love you." But nothing can take the place of those three words. How many adults have never heard those simple words from their parents?

I have sensed a great deal of suppressed rage in adult children, particularly in those from families where feelings are rarely expressed. Some parents have said, "Oh, we wouldn't applaud or compliment her. It might go to her head!" Under the guise of pseudohumility, children have been deprived of one basic ingredient for growth.

## *The threat of disinheritance*

In early American history, parents relied on the fear of dis-inheritance to keep their children in line. One major issue that was settled by the American Revolution was that the legal practices of primogeniture and entail would not be tolerated in this country. The tradition of granting everything to the oldest son or to males only was particularly offensive to Thomas Jefferson. He realized that under the traditional system, a male was at the mercy of his father. Romances were sabotaged, and marriages were arranged for the benefit of the rest of the family. As a result, many of the second or third sons had to join the army to support themselves, or find daughters of wealthy men whom they could marry. Yet a father couldn't let son number two get too far away. What would happen if the firstborn son died, especially before he produced an heir?

That was then. So what about now? You've probably heard the threats: "I'll cut you off without a cent!" the red-faced father screams at an insolent son. And, as many people know, a will can be both changed and contested.

One divorced man faced a dilemma. After his divorce was final, his father called him and explained a provision of his will: "If any of my sons divorce, his share of the estate will be divided among the other brothers. Further, his brothers may not, out of compassion, share any portion of their inheritance with him." The father explained that he had written that stip-ulation with great thought and prayer.

The son reports, "I sat there—fighting to keep my com-posure. I'd lost everything: my wife, my kids, my house, my reputation in the Christian community—and now my father was rejecting me. I knew my father was conservative, but his sense of timing devastated me."

"Why did he tell you?" I asked.

"He's open and aboveboard. Just didn't want any surprises."

"Well, fathers change their minds . . .," I suggested.

"You don't know *my* father!" he replied. This son is struggling because his father's economic rejection is only the tip of the iceberg. His dad may still send him a birthday card and a Christmas gift, but I suspect it just won't be the same anymore.

## Dangers to avoid

Some trinkets contain messages—hidden or outright. Parents may consider these long-term investments, or insurance for old age. *If I give now, he won't put me in a nursing home. Not after all I've done for him. . . .*

Some parents are simply trying to buy affection, or trying to make up for the years when they were too busy to spend much time with their children.

In 1 Samuel 20, King Saul dangled a big trinket in front of Jonathan: "As long as the son of Jesse lives on this earth, neither you *nor your kingdom* will be established" (v. 31, italics added). Saul was trying to pressure his son to unload this relationship. He could have added, "I'm only doing this for your own good."

I watched the ship *Mardi Gras* dock in Miami. I was fascinated by the process they used to get the ship tied up to the dock with those enormous ropes. They started with a thin string attached to a tennis ball. Then they tied the thin string to a bigger rope, then to a bigger rope, and then to an even bigger rope, until finally the gigantic ropes were pulled to the pier.

Few parents start with big trinkets. They begin with small, "innocent" ones. Now may be the perfect time for you to take the initiative so that you can avoid the big-ticket items that may follow.

Remember, your parents may be second-generation trinket givers. They may just be doing to you what their own parents did to them. The difference is that now the stakes and expectations are probably higher.

There is nothing wrong with accepting gifts. Be thankful that your parents can be generous. And some parents are genuinely delighted by giving. Lady Julian noted,

> A glad giver takes but little heed of the thing that he gives, but all his desire and intent is to please and solace him to whom he gives it. And if the receiver takes the gift highly and thankfully, then the courteous giver sets at nought all his cost and travail.[9]

At the same time, be careful. Some people have found it necessary to reject—gently but firmly—even the prettiest of packages. There were just too many strings attached. And some who have too quickly accepted a trinket have found that the gift was more trouble than it was worth.

Beware of parents bearing trinkets.

*Eight*

# *Break the Mold*

"Like father, like son." "Look at his old man. What can you expect?" Americans are big believers in cause and effect. We tend to blame parents for whatever problems their children have.

In Chapter 5 we showed how it is possible for parents to change. The same is true for adult sons and daughters: we *can* change.

Today we have become much more aware of how widespread a problem child abuse is. We have also discovered that many of the victimizers were themselves victimized as children. However, that does not mean that victims of child abuse or those who have been influenced in other negative ways by parents are destined to repeat the sins of their fathers and mothers.

Each of us makes *choices* to follow the example of our parents or to reject that example. Often, however, we end up throwing the baby out with the bathwater. Thus a son or daughter who was overdisciplined as a child may decide not to discipline at all. That isn't what I mean by breaking the mold; that is simply *altering* the mold.

King Saul and his son Jonathan could hardly have been more different from each other. Saul was moody, jealous, snarlish, and easily provoked. Jonathan was the opposite. Only once in 1 Samuel do we see him angry. Jonathan could have mimicked his father—after all, he was heir apparent to the throne. Moreover, it would have been to his own advantage if David had been killed. But Jonathan did not have his father's conniving nature.

By the design of God, Jonathan found much in David that appealed to his strengths. No doubt he recognized many of the same traits that he had seen his father demonstrate—at least before his heart turned sour.

This type of thing sometimes happens in a marriage. A husband sees the positive traits in his wife (as well as the negative ones). By choosing to affirm the positive aspects, he downplays (or breaks the mold) of the negative ones. That decision has to be made many times, not just once.

In a weak moment, some have snapped, "You're just like your mother!" That sets off alarms within the mate, who may have feared (or even have known) that. Suddenly, she is mentally back in childhood, struggling with her relationship with her mother. The same thing can happen in reverse, when a wife points out a connection between her husband's behavior and that of one of his parents.

Unfortunately, kissing and making up doesn't erase the painful memories that have been reawakened.

## How to break the mold

Here are some guidelines for breaking the mold and not just altering it.

*1. Recognize the mold's existence.*    Children are great imitators. If, when we were young, we saw one parent manipulate or degrade or harass the other parent, we probably practiced that same behavior on younger brothers or sisters or playmates. We experimented and gained expertise. By the time we were adults, our repertoire was well-stocked and we were confident in using the skills we had learned.

*2. Understand the mold.*   What makes a particular negative behavior effective? John heard his parents yell and scream at each other (then pull into the church parking lot and instantaneously change). John never heard them ask each other for forgiveness. Maybe that happened behind closed doors. But John vowed never to raise his voice to his wife.

So years later, when something bothered or annoyed John, he sulked and suppressed his anger, while silently praising himself for his discipline. That sulking only drove his wife up the wall. So she baited John more to get him to talk. By the time they sought counseling, they weren't talking at all. John's choice to reject his father's pattern of behavior proved to be equally destructive.

*3. Diffuse the mold.*   Some behaviors are so entrenched that they will not easily be diffused or eliminated. Yes, there may be times when you will "go for the jugular." In those moments you will need to confess that you used an old script.

Here are some steps that might help you work through disagreements effectively:

● *Stick to the subject.* So many arguments escalate into sweeping battles; it's possible to forget the original problem.

● *Never trample another's ego through sarcasm, insults, or intimidation.* It's easy to resort to sweeping generalizations, name-calling, or labeling. These again take the focus off the issue and tie it to personalities.

● *Sidestep any attempt to belittle you.* You are the custodian and chief defender of your dignity.

● *Listen.* When we do not listen, speakers become frustrated and may resort to abusive tactics, either to punish us for not listening, or to goad us into listening.

*4. Replace the mold.*    A big help in breaking the mold is to have a different role model to emulate. Listen, watch, and observe people as they communicate. Find the positive and practice it. I learned that through my mentor, John Moore, who always listened to the end of my sentences.

Few of us can or will do that. We listen to the first few words or phrases, assume we know what will follow, and then begin constructing our own response, merely waiting for the speaker to breathe. If necessary, we will interrupt.

Suppose that members of your family tend to be interruptors. The next time you interrupt someone, stop—even in mid-sentence, if necessary. Apologize. Say, "Excuse me. You were saying." The first few times you may feel awkward or stupid. Do it anyway.

Suppose that your parents were big spenders. Now, your own credit cards are charged up to the limit. You can choose to have a different life-style than your parents did.

Or your parents may have been tight with money, the kind of people who would bruise Lincoln's nose before they let go of a penny. Many sons and daughters reject that pattern, only to spend themselves into debt. You can choose your own approach that is somewhere in between.

Whatever your parents' pattern, look for the positive traits they display. Focus on those, rather than on the negative ones. If you concentrate on the negative traits, you will have a tendency to go overboard at the other extreme. It's much better to keep a positive example in front of you than a negative one.

## Understanding your parents' perspective

Many of us need to make a special effort to look at our own life-styles from our parents' perspective. Their background and experiences have shaped their values in a particular way, and we can defuse some of our resentment if we try to understand why they have problems with particular things we value.

Many times, our parents' reactions are based on fear. They may be afraid that we will change or that we will reject them. If they are over 60, they may know of other grown children who are "too busy" to be with their parents. They may fear that we will behave the same way toward them.

You may have to reject your parents' success-oriented mold: work! work! work! Steve, for example, came from a generation of doctors. Yet he wanted to be a writer, a rejection that his father took personally. Steve wanted more out of life. He wanted time. His personality was strong enough so that he could stand up to his father. Not all sons and daughters have that much courage. As a result, we have too many mediocre doctors and lawyers and writers.

In his book *Father,* Christopher Andersen tells the story of Leslie Fallon, who had not spoken to her father in almost 10 years. Her father, who owned a drugstore chain, was furious when his daughter decided to study for a master's degree in art history. "What money is there in that?" he demanded. "What a waste!" The situation was complicated by the fact that Leslie's sister had become a dentist.

Although she taught for a while, Leslie began writing for the *Los Angeles Times.* Her bylines on opera, ballet, and the symphony were read seriously. When one story made the front page, she called her father. His response was, "How much did they pay you?"

Leslie was crushed. "Newspapers don't pay free-lancers much. But I was just starting out and here I had a tremendous scoop and got a huge byline on the front page! I was thrilled, but he couldn't have cared less."[1] She has now published hundreds of articles and four books, but the hurt remains.

Some rejections are only temporary. One young man rejected his father's stale academic life for a career in the Coast Guard. But after 20 years in the service he retired and began writing. Life was not easy for the struggling black writer, but he became a household word in America when tens of millions tuned in to watch his epic, "Roots." His name is Alex Haley.[2]

## Six additional guidelines

Before you smash the mold, here are some final guidelines:

*1. Accept what you can.*    It's tempting to reject it all, but you cannot totally reject your family. We are truly free to discover ourselves only when we finally see our parents through clear lenses rather than having our vision clouded by either total devotion or total hate. We must admit that some of our families are a bewildering tangle of inconsistencies. The family on the other side of the fence may seem more appealing, but all families have their problems.

Look for the positive in your parents.

*2. Reject what you must.*    In rejecting the mold, there are those items that you must eliminate if you are going to be free to be you. Don't throw the baby out with the bathwater. Be selective, yet firm.

*3. Give it time.*    Amputation is a radical approach. Many have found a more gradual approach to be the wiser course. Some have grown frustrated in waiting for parents to change.

*4. Consider the alternatives.*    Some have found that change disappointed them. There is value to having parents who do not change. Their stability offers some measure of comfort in a world where nothing seems permanent.

*5. Be prepared to explain.*    Your parents may feel hurt by your efforts to break the mold. They know that tradition is one of the things that keeps the world going. You may have to be persistent with parents who counter, "But we've *always* done it this way!" Some have found open, candid conversation to be helpful. Your parents need to know that you are rejecting an idea or a life-style, not them.

*6. Obey God.* There will be times when God's priority in your life will be tested by your family. Parents have a habit of dragging in unrelated issues, as happened between King Saul and Jonathan. When Saul told Jonathan that his friendship toward David was bringing shame to his mother and would prevent Jonathan and his kingdom from being established, he was really saying, "If David wins out, I will be forgotten." Angrily he screamed, "Now send and bring him to me, for he must die!" (1 Sam. 20:31).

This was a terrible moment for Jonathan. He was shattered by the realization that his father was not going to change. Yet Jonathan could not obey him.

King Asa was another Old Testament figure who had to make a difficult decision about a parent. Asa could not ignore his grandmother's public idolatry: "Asa's heart was fully committed to the Lord all his life" (2 Chron. 15:17). He had to depose his grandmother from her position as queen mother.

Even Jesus had difficulties with his family members. Should *we* expect to have immunity? Jesus also said, "Do not suppose that I have come to bring peace to the earth. I did not come to bring peace, but a sword. For I have come to turn

a man against his father,
a daughter against her mother,
a daughter-in-law against her mother-in-law—
a man's enemies will be the members of his own household.

(Matt. 10:34-35)

I've never heard anyone quote that passage in front of a small group of people. It is too hard to listen to. Jesus also said, "Anyone who loves his father or mother more than me is not worthy of me; anyone who loves his son or daughter more than me is not worthy of me; and anyone who does not take his cross and follow me is not worthy of me. Whoever finds his life will lose it, and whoever loses his life for my sake will find it" (vv. 37-39).

Those are hard words indeed. They remind me of my Jewish friend Larry, who became a Christian. His father then recited the *shiva,* which officially declared that his son was dead. Larry can accept his father's attitude, but he finds that it is hard on his six-year-old son, who needs a grandfather.

Would Larry still have become a Christian if he had known all the consequences? The sparkle in his eyes answers, "Yes." Somehow, my family problems seem minor by comparison with the price Larry has had to pay to follow Jesus.

Sometimes it is painful to come to terms with the negative influences that our parents have had on us. Many adult sons and daughters would rather not acknowledge that their parents have made mistakes. They don't want to dwell on the past.

But there is a difference between acknowledging the truth about our parents and focusing on their negative qualities. The first is helpful—the second is not. In his book *Confidence,* Alan Loy McGinnis writes:

> Most parents did the best they knew how. . . . we look to the past precisely in order to make changes in our course. Only with some insight as to how we arrived at our present position can we take measures to change our direction. Insight may not solve the problem, but it is the first step.[3]

You are not bound to repeat the mistakes your parents made—unless you *choose* to repeat them.

Bill's father was a womanizer; there was always another woman in his life, and thus a wound in Bill's heart that would not heal.

The woman Bill dated was troubled by the myth, "Like father, like son." Yet Bill has chosen to accept responsibility for himself, and he has been a good and faithful husband. Why? Because he chose to break the mold.

You can make the same decision. No one knows how your life might change as a result.

# *Nine*

# *Accept Your Parents As Your Parents!*

"If only my parents were like. . . ." Have you ever used those words and filled in the blank? It's easy to look at someone else's parents and imagine how they would be as *your* parents.

One friend of mine has a famous father. As his son and I became better friends, we discussed our fathers. I assumed that he had a close relationship with his dad.

"Hardly!" he said. "He was always gone! My mom raised us by herself."

"Yeah, but he's such a spiritual giant," I insisted.

"Perhaps," he said quickly, and then changed the subject. I've never forgotten that.

Bob Benson, speaker and writer, related the story of a woman who came up to him at a conference as he was walking with his wife and daughter, yelling, "Bob Benson! Can I just touch you?"

"I wish she hadn't said that," he wrote. "I must have heard it a hundred times since then around the house. Mostly when I am getting 'uppity' about something one of the family will say, 'Bob Benson! Can I just touch you!' "[1]

## A conspiracy to honor

They say that the grass always looks greener on the other side of the fence. Some adult sons and daughters see other people's parents as the natural successors to Donna Reed, Ben Cartwright, and Ward Cleaver.

Part of the problem is that we are so afraid of disobeying the commandment to honor father and mother that we are satisfied with cosmetic relationships. These look good from the outside, but they cover up a lot of problems. The natural tendency to gloss things over is what John Trent calls a protective instinct:

Regardless of the treatment we've received as children, when we become adults, a gut-level feeling that "these are the only parents I have" seems to take over. We become more willing to forgive all parental wrongs, to cover up all sins.

We all have a tremendous God-given love for our parents, and no one should parade a parent's faults around in public. *But ignoring past problems with one's parents can prevent their cure. In fact, refusing to remember these problems is the best way to see them imitated in the present.*[2]

Before you start to covet someone else's parents, remember that you are seeing their "public" side. You do not know what it would be like to be under their roof for 24 hours or for an entire year. You have seen them in stop-frame action, like the way they freeze an Olympic runner's face on the screen as she crosses the finish line. If you were to say, "This is how she is all the time," you would be mistaken. You saw her at a particular moment and in a particular setting.

Second, some adult children "create" a father or mother. Often a prospective son- or daughter-in-law develops a quick attachment to the future spouse's parents. Think back to your first encounters with your in-laws. Have there been any surprises since then? Probably. During dating and the period of engagement, everyone is usually on their best behavior.

Third, parents change. A loss of job, a medical problem, or a "hardening of the attitudes" may significantly alter your ideal parent.

Fourth, *you* change. The type of parent you want now is probably not what you wanted 10 years ago or will want 10 years from now.

So let's take another look at the Ten Commandments. Exodus 20:17 says, "You shall not covet your neighbor's house. You shall not covet your neighbor's wife, or his manservant or maidservant, his ox or donkey, or anything that belongs to your neighbor." I like my house. I don't want my neighbor's house or wife. No one in my neighborhood has manservants or maidservants (the closest thing is lawn service). And it violates zoning laws to bring an ox or donkey into the neighborhood.

So does that put me in the clear? Almost. Unfortunately, there is that sticky little clause at the end of the commandment that says, ". . . or anything that belongs to your neighbor." And that includes my neighbor's *parents*. We have traditionally limited the scope of this commandment to tangible things like boats and cars, but parents are also included. God does not want us to covet our neighbor's parents.

## We don't choose our parents

One of the realities of life is that you can't choose your parents. You are a unique creation, the "one-flesh" fruit of two people at a particular point in their lives.

In the middle of an argument, Linda's mother suddenly blamed her for all her own unhappiness: "It's all your fault!"

"What?" Linda shouted back.

"The only reason I married your father was that I was pregnant with *you!*"

How many children have grown up with that burden to bear? That they were the glue that held their parents together in a loveless relationship?

Parents sometimes resent a particular child because of the circumstances of that child's conception. Bryan discovered that he came along "accidentally" at about the time his mother was leaving his father. He blames a lifetime of maternal abuse on that fact. "My mom said she had no place to go," so she stayed with her husband. The tension escalated year after year, until one day Bryan came home and found his father beating up his mother.

"I snapped," he said. "Afterwards, I cried as he packed his suitcase and left." Ironically, Bryan remembers that the next Sunday in church, the sermon was on honoring your father and your mother. He said, "Maybe I had honored my mother by protecting her, but that last look on my father's face as he left still haunts me."

Susan learned that she was the result of an affair—that the father she knew was not her biological father. Ever since she found out, she has fought an emotional battle, sometimes wanting to meet her real father, sometimes not. Her natural father does not know that she knows. What should she do? Does "Honor your father and your mother" mean your biological father, or the only father you have ever known? And how can you honor someone when you don't even know who he is?

Some sons and daughters come along late in their parents' lives, as "afterthoughts." Neil, for example, had parents who were older. His dad was 50 when he was born. As a busy attorney, active in service clubs and politics, he rarely had time to play ball or go fishing or camping with his son.

Neil said, "I remember wanting to have a dad like my friend Mike. When we were teens, my dad was in his late 60s. How could he play ball—even if he had wanted to? Mike's dad was still in his 30s. I felt cheated. Today, I am so awkward at sports, and I blame my dad for that!''

Perhaps your mother worked outside the home, and you wanted a mother like Mrs. Cleaver (although it always seemed strange to me that she wore heels and jewelry to mop the kitchen floor), someone who would always be there when you came home from school.

## Areas of conflict

Here are some common areas in which adult children and their parents have conflicts:

• *Liberal vs. conservative.* Many sons and daughters wish they had more liberal or "tolerant" parents. They have a tendency to think of their parents as out-of-date, in spite of the "Some day you'll thank me" speeches they have listened to.

For example, Susan wasn't allowed to go to movies or wear lipstick or jewelry. Her dresses never looked fashionable. She couldn't go to dances, ice skating, or swimming, and couldn't dance in physical education classes. But all of those things were things she wanted to do.

"It doesn't matter what other parents do. We're not *other* people!" her mother would point out.

It might not surprise you that Susan married the first guy who paid any attention to her. She saw him as a one-way ticket away from her parents. For a while, she blossomed in her marriage. But eventually she divorced her husband so that she could find out "what I have missed." Today she is an attorney, and she hasn't been in church for years. "God and my parents robbed me of my adolescence," she snaps angrily.

• *Rich vs. poor.* Americans are mixers and line-crossers. People of different economic backgrounds often socialize together or marry each other.

Rob found out about this when he went home with his college roommate over break. "It was the first time I discovered that people could have decent table conversations. I was blown away by real silver, real china, flowers, candles, and manners. I was so embarrassed. Mealtime at my house had always been a free-for-all."

During John's senior year in college he worked 40 hours a week, drove an old Chevy, and dated when he could scrape enough money together. John had a roommate who hadn't worked 40 hours during his entire four years at college. Yet he drove a new car and his parents bought him anything he wanted. John was jealous—to say the least.

But he learned that there are two sides to that coin. Some parents, although poor in possessions, are rich in nonmaterial things.

That was then. *This is now.* Now John says he wouldn't exchange places with his former roommate.

● *Applauders-rejectors.* Some parents and their sons and daughters got along fine through the teenage years and through college. But now the children are developing their own styles, tastes, and standards of living, and conflict arises.

One son described his attempt to change his father's taste buds.

"What is this?" the father demanded.

"Pâté," the son laughed.

"*Pâté?* What?" his father retorted, deliberately mispronouncing the word to barb his son. The son shrugged. Next the father had a few words to say about the prices in the restaurant where they were eating.

"I could eat for two weeks on what we're spending tonight," he said.

"Yeah," the son replied, "if you eat at fast-food city. Munch down those gut-busters."

Some families have difficulty choosing a restaurant in which everyone will feel comfortable.

For others, there are conflicts over social drinking. Among evangelicals, the issue is no longer as black and white as it once was. For many, wine is not considered offensive.

One son explained, "Sure we drink wine . . . occasionally. It's in the refrigerator. Now, my dad's not a snooper. But the other night he came for dinner, and he wanted some ketchup. 'Sit still,' he ordered. 'I'll get it.' Then I remembered the wine. So I jumped up. He jumped up.

" 'Sit still!' he ordered as if he were in his own house.

" 'No, dad,' I said, 'you're our guest.' " It got rather comical before the son retrieved the ketchup from a partially opened refrigerator door.

That's why some sons and daughters dislike unannounced visits by their parents. They may have things they don't want their parents to know about.

Gift-giving becomes the occasion for many conflicts. "Can't buy for them," one mother said. "And I sure can't surprise them."

How do you handle Christmas or birthday presents that you don't like and don't want to wear or display in your house? Do you give them away? Do you put them in the closet, and bring them out when your parents visit? When parents come over, some things may go *in* the closet, while other items come *out*.

My parents now send money, but they feel awkward about the fact that there is nothing for me to unwrap. Other parents have a standard comment that goes along with their gifts: "I kept the receipt and the tags, in case you want to take it back." It's no wonder that the day after Christmas is such a headache for stores.

Is it "honoring your parents" to pretend that you like a gift so that you won't hurt their feelings? Do your parents catch that knowing look that you exchange with your mate? If you hide your disappointment, that may only mean that the experience will be repeated next Christmas or on the next birthday.

Surely, David and Jonathan must have discussed their fathers. Jonathan must have been embarrassed about his. Perhaps he wished that his father was more like David's—or like anyone else's.

But it was not to be. Saul was Saul, and Jonathan had to accept that ugly reality.

## *Warts and all*

You may have your work cut out for you. The older you are, the more rehearsed your resentments may be, the more memories there are that you have stored away.

Once a year, on January 1, I face a big decision. Do I buy a new filing cabinet, or do I purge the current ones to make room for more folders? Considering the price of a steel, five-drawer filing cabinet, that's a relatively easy choice to make. So out come the black plastic garbage bags, and I go through each cabinet, drawer by drawer and file by file, discarding and consolidating. Sometimes I can't remember why I saved a particular newspaper article. It's amazing what I find.

I lose things in my files. It may be that you do the same thing with the memories of your parents' failures and foibles. Are they stored somewhere deep inside you? Have you forgotten what some of the issues were all about? But the sheer bulk of those memories may be filling up your memory banks with lingering pain and resentment. After the latest insult or battle, do you feel like you need to get another filing cabinet?

Maybe you, too, need to do some sorting and tossing. Do yourself a favor—even though there may have been many real injustices done to you in the past. Accept your parents as they are, warts and all. Now *that's* a great way of honoring them.

Much energy is wasted by grown sons and daughters who try to change their parents. Because of our faulty family communication patterns, we've misunderstood the word *honoring*. We've let things slide that should have been confronted. We've let the debts stack up. The burdens have gotten heavier. It's no wonder that other people's parents look better than ours do.

Maybe it's time to sing a chorus of "Auld Lang Syne" and bring out the black plastic garbage bags. Why wait for January 1? But remember, you're not making room for new garbage— new stored insults. You're letting go of the past and embracing your parents as they are.

Things can never be the way they were—but things can be *better.* God did not make your parents the way *you* would have made them. But instead of dwelling on that, look ahead. If you are a parent or someday become one, will you be the parent that your children will want?

Accepting your parents doesn't mean granting amnesty or developing a case of amnesia. It simply means saying, "That's who they are."

# Ten

# *Adjourn the Grand Jury*

Grand juries are a basic part of the American judicial system. Their task is to see if enough evidence exists to bring a person to trial. Is there a reasonableness to the charges?

Contrast these two statements about fathers:

> As a little kid, I had been defeated by my father, and have never been able to quit the battlefield all these years, despite the perpetual defeat I suffer.[1]

> These are not tears of guilt or remorse or regret. I have no bitter memories. . . . there were no harsh words that I wish I could retrieve. . . . we had no conflicts or struggles or strife. The emotion that you see reflects only the love of a son who has suddenly lost his father and gentle friend.[2]

There is quite a contrast between the two statements. The first is by Franz Kafka, the existentialist writer; the second by Dr. James Dobson.

## Grand jury indictments

What about you? How do you deal with your parents? Many people have a "sitting grand jury" before which they frequently appear to present the latest evidence against their parents—the latest insult or slight, the latest battle. It's not very surprising that the grand jury always produces an indictment.

But such a grand jury only convenes in the corridors of your mind. It is highly subjective. No wonder you always win. I wonder whether the data you use to get an indictment of your parents would stand up in a real courtroom.

Some of us have long carried deep anger over injustices that we believe our parents have committed. I think of a friend of mine, a musician, who is going deaf as a result of a medical condition that developed when he was small. Although he complained to his parents that his ears were hurting, they only laughed. He now holds them guilty for what is happening to him.

Then there is a woman in California who became involved in a premarital sexual relationship with a minister. When the scandal broke, her parents refused to support her. She "faced the music" in silence, a defiant silence. The resentment against her parents still smolders—20 years later.

Tragically, many adult sons and daughters have repressed their feelings toward their parents. As part of being "good" and "honoring" father and mother, they have denied their feelings. Some day they may realize that their closet is so full of suppressed emotions that they can no longer close the door. And then their feelings may not only come out, they may explode.

In his book *Manhood: A New Definition*. Stephen A. Shapiro offers an alternative to walking around with this kind of anger inside:

> I am grateful to my father for the gift of life. I am still engaged in the process of trying not to resent him for being who he is. I forgive him for not being all I needed him to be, and I forgive myself for wanting him to be more.[3]

We finally have to come to the conclusion that our parents did the best they could, and then we need to move on. But some adult sons and daughters will not accept that conclusion. They want justice, at the least, and in some cases, revenge. In fact, one has to wonder if some of the arguments and predicaments that adult children find themselves in are not attempts to inflict punishment on their parents through embarrassment.

Shapiro recognizes that there is a process involved in forgiving one's parents. There are no instant solutions or absolutions. In fact, some children have been too hasty to grant "immunity from prosecution" to their parents. But for others, the process is a struggle. They constantly analyze the data, continually sifting through the past, looking for clues and new evidence.

Paulette Woods, who teaches a popular seminar in this area, offers a simple suggestion: "I have tried to let him [her father] be who he is." If the problem is plural, make that, "I have finally decided to let my parents be who they are"—products of a particular generation and a particular mind-set. This means that *some parents are not going to change.*

Stella Resnick explains how some of us bring old emotional baggage into each new encounter with our parents: ". . . rather than experience each new situation (or insult) freshly and creatively, the person with a lot of unfinished business relates to the new situation with old responses."[4] Thus the past becomes a filter through which all present experiences are passed. Resnick contends,

> . . . self-responsibility means recognizing that you choose what you do and whom you are. When individuals take responsibility for their lives, they enlarge their alternatives and learn to make choices that enhance and nourish them rather than deplete them. *Blaming* other people or the situation on fate are ways in which people do not take responsibility for themselves.[5]

How about it? Are you able to let your parents be the people they are? Or have you stored up layer after layer of resentments, angers, and fears?

Some of this comes from what I call the "Big Me/Little You" syndrome. When your parent punished you, you may have mumbled something under your breath. When you were asked, "What did you say?" you lied: "Nothing." You knew that if you told the truth, you might only make the situation worse, and possibly receive more punishment.

But perhaps you were actually innocent, and it was only the circumstances of the situation that made you look guilty. When the truth came out and your innocence was discovered, your parents may not have apologized for wrongfully punishing you. And that created even more resentment.

It's true that there have been and still are a lot of parents who are ill-equipped for the task of parenting. They may attempt to preserve their authority by refusing to allow challenge of any kind. Many end discussions with, "I don't want to hear another word out of you." Words like that can have the effect of a Brillo pad on a child's delicate spirit. And some adult sons and daughters have still not forgiven their parents for that.

## Questions to consider

*1. Is it worth an indictment?*   OK, so your parents might have been wrong. But at what cost to your emotions will you pursue an indictment? And will that be enough?

Sometimes the wiser course of action is to cash in your claim checks to justice. Let the past be the past and get on with today.

*2. Are you a hostile witness?*   Are you objective in your analysis of the facts? Perhaps you were there, but you, too, have biases. And scientists have plenty of evidence to show that people tend to observe only what they expect to observe or what they *want* to observe. Frequently the problem is not that we have the facts wrong, but that we don't have *all* the facts, and we are interpreting just a few of them through our own emotional filters. The result can be a very distorted picture, even when we were eyewitnesses to something.

A television talk-show host once invited a famous trial attorney to be on his show. During the opening monologue, a man came out from the side of the stage, wearing a disguise and holding a banana in his hand. He walked around the host several times, pointed the banana at him, said, "Bang!" and then disappeared.

Afterward the attorney came out on stage and interviewed the audience to try and establish the facts of what had just happened. In spite of the fact that almost everyone in the audience had been watching the stage at the time, waiting for something to happen, these eyewitnesses disagreed on even the most basic details: how the man was dressed, what he was holding in his hand, how many times he walked around the host, and what he said.

Then the attorney made his point. If a whole studio audience of eyewitnesses couldn't agree on the details of something as simple as that, just imagine what it is like for people who weren't expecting a crime to happen to describe the details of it months—or years—later in court.

Many of us could learn a lesson from this. We may think that we know exactly what our parents did, but there could be many reasons why our interpretation might not be as accurate as we would like to think.

Some people get so wrapped up in their search for justice or vengeance that they lose their own souls and marriages. It eats away at them like cancer.

Some adult children feel crippled today because of yesterday's parental decisions. Jerome Kagan of Harvard touched off a spirited debate by publishing his book *The Nature of the Child,* in which he contended that the past is not necessarily a prelude to the future. He took issue with "the idea that parents, by the right combination of love and firmness, of mobiles and music, forever set the course of their child's life."[6]

To Professor Kagan, the way a child interprets a parental action is more important than the action itself. A child's future *is within the influence of the child* and the decisions that he or she makes. To blame mom, dad, the environment, or the lack of opportunities is to avoid full responsibility.

This explains why angry sons or daughters sometimes have a totally different perception of their parents than their siblings do. They experienced the same parents, but they made their own interpretations and choices. Our future is not dependent on whether we experienced good or bad from our parents, but rather on whether we perceive some control over that.[7]

By choosing not to convene the grand jury at the drop of a hat, you are exercising a big chunk of control and direction.

*3. Is a face-off advisable?* How long has this been brewing? Overnight? For a few months? A few years? Several decades? Maybe it's time to air the differences. Too often, parents and their adult children sit and stew or "stand back and let it fly," to use John Trent's words. Trent says that it's much more helpful to work through difficulties in an organized fashion.

Consider using Trent's strategy. First there has to be agreement on four basic rules:

● *They should set up a specific time to talk through the problem.* A time when there are a minimum of outside distractions. Twenty minutes before opening the Christmas presents is probably not a good time.

● *After they have set the time, they should keep it.*

● *They should address only one issue at a time.* There may be too many problems to solve in one sitting. If they use a shotgun-smattering approach, nothing will be resolved.

● *They should agree to use only edifying words with each other.* That means no yelling, name-calling, and hair-pulling or running away.[8]

You may be saying that this will never work in your family. Maybe in someone else's, but not in yours. But would you be willing to give it a try?

Here are Trent's three steps:

● *You should concisely explain your concern to your parents.* Hopefully, your parents will then restate what they have heard you say. Admittedly, this may be as *they* understand it, not as *you* do.

● *You should use an emotional word picture to try to explain your feelings about the issue.* A picture is worth a thousand words.

● *You should propose a workable solution to the problem.* Remember, it is just a proposal. It may sound unrealistic, but try anyway.

● *Then exchange places.* Try to think as your parents think. What motivates them? Is it fear? Insecurity?

In fact, Trent recommends that you start this process with an affirmation: "You know, mom and dad, one thing I have always appreciated about you is. . . ." Then Trent suggests three questions to consider:

● Of the solutions discussed, which one would be the best for our relationship—rather than for either me or my parents? Can we come up with a solution where neither of us loses?

● Do either of us need to ask the other's forgiveness? Did we get overly emotional or angry during the discussion? Did we exaggerate? Do we need to modify any statements?

● Do we all feel comfortable with the discussion and any decisions made? Sometimes the only solution is to agree to disagree—but the airing and listening may pave the way to harmony on other issues.[9]

Arthur Maslow and Moira Duggan noted that such conversations or confrontations push us beyond everyday ways of thinking, acting, and speaking. We must struggle to find precise words to use. They suggest,

- Say what you mean; mean what you say;
- Don't evade;
- Avoid "judgmental" or labeling words;
- Be cautious in interpreting words or actions.[10]

Remember, this is not a time for you to play psychologist or therapist. And this confrontation is an attempt to preserve the family, not destroy it.

## Ask for the Spirit's direction

Finally, I urge you to ask the Holy Spirit to direct you if you propose this alternative to your parents. If they say, "Fine. How about now?" then you should be careful about saying yes. Make sure that you are well-prepared before you confront them.

I am not certain that such a process would have worked with Saul and Jonathan. Clearly, Jonathan didn't rush to confront his father with David's accusations. On the New Moon festival, Jonathan sat across from his father. While Saul noticed David's absence from the celebration, nothing was said. However, it was the second day (and the third day since Jonathan's last conversation with David) that the confrontation took place. It was not a planned confrontation, such as the one John Trent outlines, but an angry battle (1 Sam. 20:18-34).

Are you willing to adjourn the grand jury? Are you willing to grant a pardon to your parents? A pardon means that both the accuser and the accused go free. Or will you choose to deny that a problem exists? Will you let the damage continue? Will you wait until death robs you of a chance for reconciliation? Alan Loy McGinnis says,

One of my clients, who is in her seventies and has retired from a successful sales career, had to begin seeing a therapist because she dreams of her mother almost every night, and is plagued by unresolved issues with her parents. Her mother has been dead for 51 years.[11]

Quite frankly, I am not concerned about families that shout and scream and pound tables nearly as much as I am about families who refuse to raise their voices, to confront issues, who allow themselves to be suffocated by unresolved conflicts.

In the legal world there are times when a prosecutor is convinced that he or she has an airtight case. Open and shut. Yet for one of many reasons, the prosecutor may choose not to bring the case to trial. It isn't always worth the time, expense, and effort.

The same thing can be said about many of the cases that adult children build against their parents. It might be possible to indict them, but that really isn't the answer. What is needed instead is forgiveness.

Charles Wesley wrote these powerful words to one of his hymns:

He breaks the power of cancelled sin
He sets the prisoner free.
His blood can make the foulest clean
His blood availed for me.

That phrase, "the power of cancelled sin," includes the power of our memories—that desire to rehash, to seek a pound of flesh for an ounce of infraction, that need for justice to be meted out.

It's difficult to pray, "O God, help my family," when you are always placing new items in the file folders—when you are always "making a list and checking it twice."

Today could be a good day to adjourn the grand jury—to grant a pardon—to devise a way to overcome the estrangement between you and your parents.

# A Season Called Suffering, a Moment Called Death

An old Jewish proverb says, "Every man knows he will die, but no one wants to believe it." Parents do get older, perhaps become ill, and finally die. That sequence has a profound impact on their children as well. In some cases it means increased responsibility. It may even mean a complete role reversal, in which the child becomes "parent" and the parent becomes "child."

In the last several years I have had to deal with my own father's aging and his medical problems related to that. At times, I feel like the angel of death is tardy. My dad has nephritis, heart trouble, skin cancer, and is locked on a kidney dialysis machine three days a week. He also recently had a serious heart attack. He was once a large man; now he is tiny and frail. The man who could once work 18-hour days is now barely able to walk a few steps.

It has broken my heart. I have lain on my floor and cried. I sat with him by the Christmas tree last year and he whispered, "I didn't think I'd be around for this one." My sister said,

"Daddy, it wouldn't be Christmas without you." We all looked at each other in a wordless moment.

When it was time for me to go to the airport, he was too weak even to ride along in the car. I hugged his neck and he said, "I'm sorry I can't go with you." That was the first time I remember my father ever saying he was sorry for anything.

"If there's anything of mine that you want," he said, "just take it."

"Daddy," I answered, fighting for composure, "the only thing I want is for you to get well." Immediately, his eyes became very alert.

"That isn't going to happen!" he said with quiet certainty.

I started to say, "Sure it is," but the look he gave me stopped me short. I simply nodded.

My father is not going to get well or even better. He will only get worse, until the tardy angel of death calls at his door.

I hugged my dad and told him I loved him. Finally I pulled away, as if to memorize the moment. Those pleading eyes said volumes. What had happened to my big, strong daddy who was always there to protect me? The one who had worked so hard to keep me fed? Who had gone without to help me go to college?

I cried on the way to the airport. I cried on the plane that took me home. How could life be so cruel?

These days I hold my breath when the phone rings in the night, or if I arrive at a church to speak and someone says, "There's a long distance phone call for you. It sounded important."

It is only a matter of time until I say that last good-bye. But there is still a lot of unfinished business in my heart. And I have discovered, as did Mark Twain, that the years make our parents so much more lovable and smart. For the suffering my dad has endured has taken the rough edges off him. There is an almost incredible sense of gentleness about him now.

Part of the pain I experience is very personal. My dad has my mom, my brothers and sisters, grandchildren, and great-grandchildren to "be there." But what about me? I'm single. Who will be there when I am old? When I am feeble? When I am weak and waiting to die?

It has helped me somewhat to realize that there are no assurances of someone "being there," even for married people. My dad has my mom, but my mom will probably not have my dad. And this year, 110,000 divorces will occur among individuals over the age of 55, and 12,000 divorces to those over 65.[1]

Perhaps you feel squeezed between the generations. You may be middle-aged, with elderly parents and adolescent or college-age children. In your parents' aging you may feel that somehow your own life is escaping.

While the financial drain can be enormous, the emotional strain can be just as hard to bear. Francine Klagsbrun noted that frequently there is ". . . anger at parents for being old and sick and guilt at never being able to do enough, meaning that you're not able to save them from death."[2]

## How do we cope?

The death of a parent leaves a large, empty space in the life of an adult son or daughter. How can we deal with this reality? Here are some suggestions:

*1. Recognize that change is inevitable.*   In general, we Americans do not handle death well. We use special words and special tones of voice to disguise our fear. One friend was told of his father's death by someone who said, "He's gone."

" 'Gone'?" my friend asked. "He's sick. Where's he gone?" The next statement was that he had "expired."

"Are you trying to tell me that he's dead?" my friend asked? When the answer was yes, he said, "Then why didn't you say so?"

*2. Prepare yourself to deal with the reality of death.*   The approach of death causes people to change. They want to pack their last months, weeks, and days with pleasant memories. In some cases, that means clearing up "old business."

On the one hand, you may welcome the change, but still resent it. You wanted your parents to change by their own choice, not because they were being stampeded by the fear of death.

Maybe life is merciful in giving us time to say our goodbyes. In my family I was often told, "Don't leave without saying good-bye." But sometimes death catches us by surprise.

When I worked as a funeral director, I saw grown children weeping beside caskets, lamenting that it was too late to say some things they had wanted to say.

The death of a parent is hard on children. But living with their dying can be even harder. Watching parents slowly decline in health, both mental and physical, is part of the emotional anguish that many adult children must face. Sometimes they think they will go crazy.

One psychologist told about her mother: "I'll be having such a good day. Then mom will walk in here and ask, 'Isn't that my sweater you have on?' Or she had left her car here with us while she went on a trip. The kids decided to wash it and clean it from top to bottom. They worked so hard on it. She took one look and began complaining about the fender. 'Billy had a wreck in my car!' I couldn't convince her that he had not even driven it. That dent had been there for years. But I had to deal with Billy. Not only had his grandmother accused him of wrecking her car, she accused him of lying about it. He was devastated. He just couldn't understand her."

*3. Focus on the positive.*   Yes, your parents have many foibles. And as they age, these may become more pronounced. They may also develop new ones. But look for the positive qualities that are there, and enjoy those.

*4. Savor the opportunities.*   It is important to spend time listening to your parents as they write the concluding chapter of their lives. Listen to the ends of their sentences and paragraphs. Listen to what is *not* said as well as to what *is* said. *Listen.*

*5. Be prepared for personal change.*   The death of a parent may bring significant change to you as well. For some, a parent's death is a time for a new commitment to faith in Christ. For others, it prompts a fresh start or a resolve to take more time for things that are really important.

When death comes, remember Paul's words: "Where, O death, is your victory? Where, O death, is your sting?" Paul proclaimed confidently, "Thanks be to God! He gives us the victory through our Lord Jesus Christ" (1 Cor. 15:55, 57).

Death is not the ending, but a beginning. And it is possible that you will die before your parents do. That makes it even more important to take the initiative now in making peace with your parents. You might find it helpful to imagine what it would be like if either you or your parents were to die six months from now. What are the things that you would have wished you had done before that happened? Don't wait until it's too late. Make a start *now*.

# Taking the First Step

In the parable of the Prodigal Son, Jesus said that while the son "was still a long way off, his father saw him and was filled with compassion for him" (Luke 15:20). That verse may describe where you are in making peace with your family: it's "still a long way off."

Building an adult relationship with your parents is not something you do in one day. It may require a lifetime. It can be painful, lonely, and disheartening. But I would ask you to consider two questions:

- If not me, then *who*?
- If not now, then *when*?

Coming to terms with your parents is part of the agenda of adulthood. But remember, your task is not to chastise or punish your parents. Donald S. Williamson adds, "Nor is it to demand or need them to be in any way different." Rather, it is a son or daughter's ability to "embrace the first generation *exactly* as they are."[1]

There are delicate balances of power that must be maintained in order to ensure the safety of the world, especially among the superpowers. There are checks and balances that are necessary among the three branches of the federal government to ensure stability and tranquility. Similarly, there are delicate balances of power necessary to ensure domestic tranquility in a family.

It is possible for you to have a healthy family with *distinct boundaries*. There can be closeness within the boundaries when the relationship between parents and adult children is *freely chosen* rather than an expression of obligation.

Too many of us have grown up with a debtor vs. collector approach to family relationships: "After all I've done for you . . ." is the magic phrase. Too often, loyalties to parents are fueled by motivations such as:

- a sense of indebtedness
- a sense of fear
- a sense of intimidation
- a sense of powerlessness

These are not the kinds of motivations that will produce healthy relationships.

There's a lot of construction going on in my city as I write this book. In fact, my own home and that of my neighbor are being remodeled. Sometimes things have to be torn down, ripped away, and altered in order to make way for the new.

But my advice for you is, *Go slow in the change process.* Change what you can. Live with the rest.

You could begin the process of change by taking a look at the way you are communicating with your parents. Are you:

- talking *to* them?
- talking *at* them?
- talking *with* them?

A Chinese proverb puts it succinctly: "The journey of a thousand miles begins with but a single step." Your first step begins with an admission that your family is not perfect.

Sometime, when you have an hour, take a walk and carefully consider these questions:

What are some things that are important to my parents?

What makes my parents care?

What gives my parents hope? What makes them anxious?

What is the meaning of their work?

Where does their pain lie?

What are their expectations for me? for my children? for my brothers and sisters?

What makes them speak out on a subject?

What are their weaknesses?

What are their unrealized dreams?

What are their strengths?

Am I willing to let them be my parents, warts and all?

# *Notes*

## "How Do We 'Honor Father and Mother' Today?"

1. Elena Latici, "Who's the Nice One, Or the Smart One, Or the Bossy One in Your Family?" *Redbook,* November 1985, p. 110.
2. Jerome Kagan, *The Nature of the Child* (New York: Basic Books, 1984), p. 280.
3. Eugene Kennedy, *Sexual Counseling: A Practical Guide for Non-Professional Counselors* (New York: Continuum, 1977), pp. ix-x.
4. Michele Slung, *Momilies: As My Mother Used to Say* (New York: Ballantine, 1985), p. 1.
5. Howard Halpern, *Cutting Loose: An Adult Guide to Coming to Terms with Parents* (New York: Bantam, 1977), pp. 82-91.
6. *Ibid.*, p. 83.
7. *Ibid.*, p. 92.

## "Overcoming the Five Fears"

1. Carolyn Koons, lecture on change, July 28, 1985.
2. Harry Petrakis, *Reflections* (Chicago: Lake View, 1983), pp. 92-93.

## Chapter 1. "Choose To Be a Son or a Daughter"

1. Herbert S. Stream, *The Sexual Dimension* (New York: Free Press, 1983).
2. Wayne Dyer and John Vriend, *Group Counseling for Personal Mastery* (New York: Cornerstone, 1982), p. 31.
3. Herb Goldberg, *The Hazards of Being Male: Surviving the Myth of Masculine Privilege* (New York: Nash, 1976), pp. 180-181.
4. Robert J. Havinghurst, *Developmental Tasks and Education,* 3rd ed. (New York: Longman, 1972), pp. 83-94.
5. Carole Klein, *Mothers and Sons* (Boston: Houghton Mifflin, 1984), p. 115.
6. *Ibid.,* p. 236.
7. Claire Bishop Barton, "Hi, Mom! We're Back!" *Newsweek,* August 9, 1982, p. 8.

## Chapter 2. "Reject Your Parents' Fears and Irrationalities"

1. Meredith Tax, *Rivington Street* (New York: William Morrow, 1982), pp. 208-209.
2. Denis Waitley and Reni L. Witt, *The Joy of Working* (New York: Dodd, Mead, 1985), pp. 207-208.

## Chapter 3. "Determine Your Territorial Waters"

1. Zenith Henkin Gross, *And You Thought It Was All Over: Mothers and Their Adult Children* (New York: St. Martins, 1985), p. 148.
2. *Ibid.,* p. 142.
3. John T. Trent, *Growing Together* (Wheaton, Ill.: Victor, 1985), p. 84.

## Chapter 5. "Resist Your Parents' Curiosity"

1. Gross, *And You Thought It Was All Over,* p. 148.

## Chapter 6. "Regulate Your Time Together"

1. Gross, *And You Thought It Was All Over,* p. 133.
2. *Ibid.,* p. 51.

3. "When Was the Last Time You Called Your Mother?" *New York,* May 7, 1979, pp. 47-54.
4. *Ibid.,* p. 48.
5. Lillian E. Troll, "Family Life in Middle and Old Age: The Generation Gap," *Annals of the American Academy of Political and Social Science* 464 (November 1982): 44.
6. Trent, *Growing Together,* p. 43.

## Chapter 7. "Duck the Trinkets"

1. Paula and Dick McDonald, *Guilt Free* (New York: Ballantine, 1977), p. 318.
2. Joseph Lash, *Eleanor and Franklin* (New York: Norton, 1971), p. 162.
3. *Ibid.,* p. 643.
4. Benjamin Kearney, *Anna Eleanor Roosevelt: Evolution of a Reformer* (New York: Houghton Mifflin, 1968), p. 15.
5. *Ibid.,* p. 247; Tamara K. Hareven, *Eleanor Roosevelt: An American Conscience* (Chicago: Quadrangle, 1968), pp. 13-14.
6. Ralph W. Bullock, *In Spite of Handicaps* (Freeport, N.Y.: Books for Libraries, 1968), pp. 100-105.
7. Kearney, *Anna Eleanor Roosevelt,* p. 16.
8. *Ibid.,* p. 247.
9. Helene S. Arnstein, *Getting Along with Your Grown-up Children* (New York: M. Evans, 1970), p. 173.

## Chapter 8. "Break the Mold"

1. Christopher P. Andersen, *Father: The Figure and the Force* (New York: Warner, 1983), p. 198.
2. *Ibid.,* pp. 203-204.
3. Alan Loy McGinnis, *Confidence: How to Succeed at Being Yourself* (Minneapolis: Augsburg, 1987), p. 113.

## Chapter 9. "Accept Your Parents As *Your* Parents!"

1. Bob Benson, *He Speaks Softly* (Waco, Tex.: Word, 1985), p. 125.
2. Trent, *Growing Together,* p. 44.

## Chapter 10. "Adjourn the Grand Jury"

1. Quoted by Klein in *Mothers and Sons*, p. 34.
2. James Dobson Jr., "Tribute To My Father," *Herald of Holiness*, June 15, 1978, p. 20.
3. Stephen A. Shapiro, *Manhood: A New Definition of Masculinity* (New York: Putnam, 1984), p. 36.
4. Stella Resnick, "Gestalt Therapy: The Hot Seat of Personal Responsibility," *Psychology Today*, November 1974, pp. 111-117.
5. *Ibid.*, p. 111.
6. Jerome Kagan, "What Shapes the Child?" *Newsweek*, October 1, 1984, p. 59.
7. Klein, *Mothers and Sons*, p. 217.
8. Trent, *Growing Together*, pp. 98-101.
9. *Ibid.*
10. Arthur Maslow and Moira Duggan, *Family Connections: Parenting Your Grown Children* (New York: Doubleday, 1982), p. 178.
11. Alan Loy McGinnis, *Confidence: How to Succeed at Being Yourself* (Minneapolis: Augsburg, 1987), p. 108.

## "A Season Called Suffering, a Moment Called Death"

1. Barbara S. Cain, "The Gray Divorcee," *Courier-Journal Magazine*, February 20, 1983.
2. Colleen Leahy Johnson and Donald J. Caralano, "Childless Elderly and Their Support Systems," *The Gerontologist* 21:617.

## "Taking the First Step"

1. Donald S. Williamson, "Personal Authority in Family Experience Via Termination of the Intergenerational Hierarchical Boundary: A New Stage in the Family Life Cycle," *Journal of Marriage and Family Therapy*, October 1981, p. 444.

# Recommended Resources

Bloomfield, Harold H., and Felder, Leonard. *Making Peace with Your Parents*. New York: Ballantine, 1985.

Ehrenreich, Barbara. *The Hearts of Men: American Dreams and the Flight from Commitment*. New York: Doubleday, 1984.

Jensen, Mary, and Jensen, Andrew. *Making Your Marriage Work*. Minneapolis: Augsburg, 1985.

Meredith, Don. *Who Says Get Married? How to Be Happy and Single*. Nashville: Thomas Nelson, 1981.

Muto, Susan Annette. *Celebrating the Single Life*. New York: Doubleday, 1982.

O'Kane, Monica Lauen. *Living with Adult Children: A Helpful Guide for Parents and Grown Children Sharing the Same Roof*. St. Paul: Diction, 1982.

Raines, Robert A. *Going Home*. New York: Crossroad, 1985.

# Also by
# Harold Ivan Smith

*Help for Parents of a Divorced Son or Daughter.* St. Louis: Concordia, 1981.

*I Wish Someone Understood My Divorce: A Practical Cope-Book.* Minneapolis: Augsburg, 1986.

*Life-Changing Answers to Depression.* Eugene, Ore.: Harvest House, 1985.

*More Than "I Do": An Engaged Couple's Premarital Handbook.* Kansas City: Beacon Hill, 1983.

*Pastoral Care for Single Parents.* Kansas City: Beacon Hill, 1982.

*Positively Single.* Wheaton: Victor, 1986.

*Tear Catchers.* Nashville: Abingdon, 1984.

*Priscilla and Aquila.* (Coauthored with Lois T. Henderson.) San Francisco: Harper and Row, 1985.